The GOSPEL of MARK

The Gospel of Mark
A Beginner's Guide to the Good News

The Gospel of Mark
978-1-7910-2483-3
978-1-7910-2484-0 *eBook*

The Gospel of Mark DVD
978-1-7910-2487-1

The Gospel of Mark: Leader Guide
978-1-7910-2485-7
978-1-7910-2486-4 *eBook*

Also by Amy-Jill Levine

Entering the Passion of Jesus:
A Beginner's Guide to Holy Week

Light of the World:
A Beginner's Guide to Advent

Sermon on the Mount:
A Beginner's Guide to the Kingdom of Heaven

The Difficult Words of Jesus:
A Beginner's Guide to His Most Perplexing Teachings

Witness at the Cross:
A Beginner's Guide to Holy Friday

Signs and Wonders:
A Beginner's Guide to the Miracles of Jesus

AMY-JILL LEVINE

The GOSPEL of MARK

A BEGINNER'S GUIDE to the GOOD NEWS

Abingdon Press | Nashville

The Gospel of Mark
A Beginner's Guide to the Good News

Library of Congress Control Number: 2023936031
978-1-7910-2483-3

Scripture quotations that appear in italics are the author's own translations.

Scripture quotations not in italics and not otherwise noted are taken from the New Revised Standard Version Updated Edition (NRSVue). Copyright © 2021 National Council of Churches of Christ in the United States of America. Used by permission. All rights reserved worldwide.

Scripture quotations marked (NIV) are taken from the Holy Bible, New International Version®, NIV®. Copyright © 1973, 1978, 1984, 2011 by Biblica, Inc.™ Used by permission of Zondervan. All rights reserved worldwide. www.zondervan.com The "NIV" and "New International Version" are trademarks registered in the United States Patent and Trademark Office by Biblica, Inc.™

Scripture quotations marked KJV are from the King James Version, which is in the public domain.

Source texts for the works of Josephus can be found at Sefaria.org: https://www.sefaria.org/texts/Second%20Temple/Josephus.

MANUFACTURED IN THE UNITED STATES OF AMERICA

For Julia Tanner

CONTENTS

INTRODUCTION

The Gospel of Mark, considered by most scholars to be the earliest canonical Gospel, is shorter than the Gospels of Matthew, Luke, and John. Unlike the other three Gospels, Mark's text offers no account of Jesus's origins and no Resurrection appearances. Instead, Mark's Gospel starts with the preaching of John the Baptizer, and it ends, at least in its earliest manuscripts, with three women fleeing the empty tomb in fear. Most biblical scholars agree that the evangelists we call Matthew, Luke, and John not only used Mark's Gospel as a source but also supplemented and even sought to correct it. When the Gospel of Luke (1:1) speaks of the many who have attempted to compile an orderly account of the story of Jesus, the writer most likely had Mark in mind.

This study seeks to learn from and about the Gospel of Mark on its own terms, without the details the other three Gospels introduce. Going chapter by chapter rather than by themes (discipleship, Christology, miracles, etc.) allows us better to experience Jesus's complex identity: at one point unable to do mighty works because of people's unbelief and at another walking on the water as only God can do; at one point demanding that people not announce his miracles; and at another clearly announcing his death and resurrection. This progressive approach helps readers to answer the question Jesus asks his disciples midway through, *Who do you say that I am?* (lit. *Who do you say me to be?*)(Mark 8:29). The answer may change at the end of each chapter. When we reread Mark's Gospel, the answer may change again, just as our sense of our loved ones changes over time.

Since we cannot cover every story, this volume features in-depth studies of select passages that I have not elsewhere discussed in this series. I have provided my own fairly literal translations from the Greek and Hebrew in order to allow hearing the stories anew (these translations appear in italics). They may seem choppy—and they are. But what they do is show where in the Greek sentences terms appear, stick more closely to the Greek than English translations that smooth over Mark's occasionally awkward syntax, and remind us all that we are reading a work that was written two thousand years ago You are encouraged to read along with your own Bible. Comparing my literal translation to your English versions will help you focus on hearing the text as if for the first time. And that's not a bad thing.

The chapters locate these passages in their historical context, develop their connections to the Old Testament (the Christian Bible, Part 1), and show how they impact both the events that follow and give added perspective into what is earlier described. This study reveals how the Gospel of Mark spoke to its earliest audiences and how it continues to speak to readers, including me, today.

Initial Questions, Illusive Answers

Who wrote this Gospel? We don't know. All four canonical Gospels were originally anonymous. Early Christian tradition regards Mark as the "John Mark" who accompanied Peter, until he didn't (see Acts 12:12; 15:37-39). Therefore, we'll call the author "Mark." Were I Peter, I might be inclined to sue Mark for defamation, given his generally negative presentation: we'll keep watch for Peter, who emerges in this Gospel as a failed disciple. Yet we know from the other Gospels, from Paul's letters, and from post-biblical tradition that Peter, after denying Jesus, became one of the leaders of the communities gathered in Jesus's name. Already we glimpse Mark's genius: Mark gives us the first half of a story, up to Peter weeping upon hearing the cock crow after he three times denies Jesus. It is our responsibility to continue the story, to move from despair into hope and from death into new life. Similarly, Mark leaves us at the empty tomb; it is our task to bring resurrection to the story of Jesus and find new life for ourselves as we read, and reread.

When was Mark's Gospel written? The text dates to the first century, probably after the Romans torched the Jerusalem Temple in 70 CE. Where? Tradition locates Mark's Gospel in Rome. The first Epistle of Peter (I doubt Peter the apostle wrote this text, but that's another story) states, *She in Babylon, elect together with you, sends you greetings; and so does my son Mark* (1 Peter 5:13; most English translations gloss that unidentified "she" with something like "sister church"; that "she" could be a woman; again, another story for another time). Another tradition sees the Gospel as originating in Egypt, since Mark was considered the first bishop appointed there. Other suggestions include Upper Galilee and Syria.

You can determine for yourselves whether the location would matter. For example, were Mark writing in the wake of Nero's scapegoating of Christians for the great fire in 64 in Rome, the Gospel's first readers may have understood Jesus's own suffering as mirroring theirs. But Mark's import was not, and is not, restricted to whatever an initial audience may have heard. Mark, like the other Gospel writers, likely addressed anyone willing to listen.

Even why Mark wrote remains speculative, and Mark may have had multiple motives: to preserve the memories of Jesus as the first generation of followers died; to focus on Jesus's suffering rather than his miracles; to show that outsiders—a Syro-Phoenician woman, an unnamed woman who anoints Jesus, a centurion guarding the cross—can be more faithful than insiders such as the twelve disciples or the women who followed Jesus from Galilee to Jerusalem; to encourage perseverance despite despair, rejection, persecution, even death.

When I first started studying the Bible (for an approximate date on that, when Noah was on the ark), my professors told me the Gospels of Matthew and John were written to Jewish followers of

Jesus, and those of Mark and Luke were addressed to Gentiles. Today, biblical scholars are much more cautious. The arguments for positing a gospel "community" are circular: we read text, we construct the intended audience based on what we've read, and then we interpret the text based on the construction. Circular arguments are always problematic. Mark clearly has Gentile Jesus-followers in mind since Mark explains, sometimes incorrectly, Jewish customs; but I suspect Mark would be delighted were anyone, whether Jew or Samaritan or Gentile, to read this Gospel.

Upshot: Mark's Gospel was written, in Greek, somewhere around or after the year 70, in the Roman Empire. That Mark's is the earliest of the extant Gospels (others may have been lost to history) does not mean that Mark's Gospel is the most accurate with respect to recording what Jesus said or did. The other evangelists may have had access to other earlier or better sources. Further, all the evangelists have their own agendas: they are not simply recording what they heard; they are also writing to develop the faith of their readers and to promote particular understandings of who Jesus is and what it means to follow him.

Had Jesus's followers not been interested in different perspectives, they could have combined all four Gospels into one continuous narrative, as did the second-century Syrian Christian Tatian in his *Diatesseron* (Greek: "through four, one") and as do most Christmas pageants (with Matthew's magi and Luke's shepherds), Passion Narratives (with the famous seven last words of Jesus, taken from all four Gospels), or Resurrection stories (Matthew's Great Commission, Luke's appearance of Jesus to two disciples on the Road to Emmaus; John's Mary Magdalene at the tomb and doubting Thomas).

When I ask my students to tell me what parts of the Gospels they find most memorable or most interesting, few if any cite material from Mark. Popular is Matthew 5–7, the "Sermon on the Mount." In Mark's Gospel, Jesus teaches more by actions than by words.

Many cite Luke's compassionate Jesus who says, *Blessed are you poor* (6:20), tells the parables of the good Samaritan and prodigal son, and prays from the cross, *Father, forgive them* (23:34). I picture Luke's Jesus extending his arms and welcoming people into his embrace. Mark's Jesus is more likely to glare in frustration (grading papers often makes me feel the same way), whether at demons who promote their own kingdom or at disciples who miss his points repeatedly.

Some cite Jesus's self-revelation in John's Gospel, *I am the True Vine* (15:1) .... *I am the Bread of Life* (6:35) .... *I am the Way, and the Truth, and the Life* (14:6), and the famous John 3:16, *For in this way God loved the world that his Son, the only begotten Son, he gave.* Mark's Jesus is less self-revelatory than secretive; he often tells those whom he has healed *not* to make this news public. Mark's Jesus does not say anything "plainly" until chapter 8, midway through the Gospel, when he announces his forthcoming death.

Mark is an acquired taste: savor it slowly, let it lead, and let it challenge.

> **Mark is an acquired taste: savor it slowly, let it lead, and let it challenge.**

The Beginning

The Gospel of Mark begins, *Beginning.* All words matter, especially for texts that were designed to be read aloud and that had to be copied by hand. The Greek for "beginning" is *archē,* as in archaeology. The Septuagint (abbreviated LXX, for "seventy" given the legend of seventy translators who prepared the Greek text from the Hebrew original), the Greek translation of Israel's Scriptures—what Jews eventually called the Tanakh and Christians the Old Testament—starts, *In the beginning (en archē)* (Genesis 1:1). Mark's opening invokes Genesis. We'll hear such echoes of that text throughout the Gospel.

The two next words in Mark 1:1 are *tou euangeliou, of the good news* or *of the gospel. Tou* is easy; it's the genitive (the possessive form of the direct article "the"). Now, we've got a problem. There's an old Italian saying, *Traduttore, traditore,* literally, "translator, traitor." Every translator chooses among options. The Greek term, in the nominative form, is *euangelion. Eu* is "good," as in eulogy and euphemism. *Angelion,* whence "angel," means "news" or "message"; an angel is, by job description, a "messenger." Thus, Mark's third word is, literally "good news."

Mark again echoes the Septuagint. Isaiah 40:9 offers a *herald of good news (euangelizomenos,* a participle), and the good news in this verse is, "Here is your God." The term reappears in Isaiah 52:7, which in the Greek reads, *like the feet of one bringing good news (euangelizomenos), of a report of peace, like the one bringing good news (euangelizomenos) of good things, because I will make your salvation heard, saying to Zion, 'Your God will reign.'*

For ancient Israel, salvation did not mean an eternal blessed afterlife. It meant salvation from this-worldly dangers: slavery, illness, war, famine, or drought. Salvation was palpable. So, too, for the Gospels, the message of salvation, the good news, must be more than a postmortem fate. Salvation also occurs in the here-and-now.

> **So, too, for the Gospels, the message of salvation, the good news, must be more than a postmortem fate. Salvation also occurs in the here-and-now.**

For Mark's contemporaries, *euangelion* was a secular term; it was good news, usually of the political sort: the "good news" of the emperor's birthday, for example, often came with tax relief or gifts to the poor. However, thanks in no small measure to Mark, the term very early became associated with the story of Jesus. The Greek term comes into Latin as *evangelium* (whence "evangelical") and then into Old English as *god* (i.e., "good") + *spel* (i.e., spiel, or story/news), whence "gospel." Thus, Mark opens with either *[The] beginning of the good news of...* or *[The] beginning of the Gospel of....* Mark will use *euangelion* six more times (1:14, 15; 8:35; 10:29; 13:10; 14:9; and in the appendix, 16:15). With each use comes additional nuance. Mark again offers an invitation: What "good news" do we find with each story, and then how do we find "good news" as we leave the empty tomb and carry the story forward?

The next words are *Iēsou Christou,* "Of Jesus Christ." Again, a translation problem. (Don't worry; we won't stop at every word!) Jesus's name, in Aramaic, would have been something like Yeshua, from the same Hebrew root as the names Joshua and Hosea, or the term "hosannah," which people shout as Jesus enters Jerusalem (Mark 11:9); it means "Save Now!" or "Save, please!" "Christ" is a Greek word that translates the Hebrew *meshiach,* which means "anointed." *Meshiach* can also be translated "Messiah."

> **When we read Mark's Gospel, we shall need to determine what kind of Christ, what kind of Messiah, Jesus is.**

Do we read Jesus Christ? Jesus Anointed? Jesus Messiah? All are correct, but each has a different nuance. Christ, which is not a last name (I've had students think that Jesus is the son of Mary and Joseph Christ), has the connotation of "lord" or "savior." "Anointed" suggests a commission for a particular task: kings and priests were anointed. *Meshiach* or "messiah" connotes, at least in the Hebrew, less a divine being who saves from sin and death and more a human being who announces the in-breaking of the messianic age signaled by the general resurrection of the dead followed by a final judgment and then peace on earth. Thus, when we read Mark's Gospel, we shall need to determine what kind of Christ, what kind of Messiah, Jesus is.

Compared to contemporaneous literature, Mark's Gospel looks like a biography (the technical term is *bios*, or a "life," as in the term "bio-logy"). Suetonius wrote *Lives of the Twelve Caesars*, Philo of Alexandria wrote *Life of Moses*, and Mark was, as far as extant sources go, the first to write a Life of Jesus. In antiquity, people wrote "Lives" less to record what happened and more to provide moral guidance: some biographies depict what an honorable person says or does, so that the "life" serves as a model to be imitated; some depict what a dishonorable person does, so that the "life" serves as the model to be avoided.

For Mark, Jesus the Christ who suffers and dies is the model to follow, hard as that path may be. Mark does not paper over the difficulties of discipleship. Jesus speaks plainly when he teaches, *If any wishes after me to follow, let that one deny himself [or herself] and take up his [or her] cross and follow me* (Mark 8:34; I've included "herself" and "her" because Jesus's followers, and Mark's readers, have never been only men). To take up the cross is to be willing to risk death, indeed to die, for the cause. Mark is not suggesting that disciples court martyrdom; no one, not even Jesus, wants to be put to death. Rather, Mark shows how to face death, with grief and anger, but also with trust and hope.

The last two words of 1:1—*huiou theou*, meaning "Son of God"—are also problematic, but not only because of translation. The first problem is that these words do not occur in all major ancient manuscripts. Since it's easier to explain why scribes added these terms to reinforce Jesus's divine status than to explain why scribes would have omitted the words, many scholars think that Mark did not begin by identifying Jesus as the Son of God. Rather, copyists thought Jesus needed something more at the outset than the title "Anointed One," or "Messiah," which would not initially have held much meaning for Gentile (that is, pagan) readers. The second problem is whether to capitalize "son" in the expression "son of God." Ancient Greek does not give us the convention of capitalizing proper names or titles, so the choice is ours. The capital "S" indicates a divine being; the lowercase "s" does not.

The title "son of god" is known from Greek and Roman texts: Hercules, Perseus, Theseus, as well as Alexander the Great, Augustus Caesar, and lots of other figures were technically "sons of" one god or another. The previous sentence also shows the problem with capitalization. We do not typically capitalize "god" in referring to Zeus or Odin, but we do in referring to the "God" of the Bible. Hence theology impacts grammar. For ancient Israel, "son of God" was especially associated with the Davidic kingship. Psalm 2:7 (LXX), for example, a "royal psalm," states, *The Lord said to me, 'My son you are; I today have begotten you.'* Psalm 89, another royal psalm, reads in the Greek translation, *He himself will call me, 'My Father you are, my God, and the upholder of my salvation!' And I a firstborn will appoint him, the highest of the kings of the earth* (Psalm 89:26-27/ LXX Psalm 88:27-28).

So far, we have a beginning, something new but something that also concerns the Book of Genesis. We have "good news," but the content is vague: Good news for whom? Regarding what? Now or in the future or both? "Son of God" may have something to do with Davidic kingship as well as appeal to Gentile readers who know of heroes with divine paternity. As we work our way through the Gospel, we'll find more allusions to the Scriptures of Israel, a developing sense of the good news in terms of exorcism and healings, provision of food, and a death whose meaning we readers must determine for ourselves.

Where Are We Going?

For the rest of this introduction, we'll see how Mark begins to tease out the contents of this "good news." It cannot be only that Jesus dies as a *ransom for many* (Mark 10:45), since Jesus will not die until chapter 15. Indeed, Mark may have written a Gospel to supplement Paul's letters, since Paul makes much of Jesus's death and resurrection but in his letters says very little about his life. Mark's good news begins with the preaching of John the Baptizer, Jesus's own baptism and temptation, the calling of his first disciples, and several healing stories. For this introduction, we'll develop those first several verses about John.

> **Mark's good news begins with the preaching of John the Baptizer, Jesus's own baptism and temptation, the calling of his first disciples, and several healing stories.**

For chapter 1, as with all the chapters in this book, we must choose which among Mark's numerous stories to highlight. Chapter 1, which covers the rest of Mark 1–4, looks first at John the Baptizer. Here we address Mark's repurposing of ancient Israel's prophecies, the question of Jesus's sinlessness, and the role of repentance. We turn then to the call of Levi the tax collector, and what it would have meant for Jesus and his contemporaries to associate with tax collectors. We'll talk about fasting, a ritual still practiced by Jews, Christians, and many others; and we'll develop this point in terms of how we often misunderstand the practices of different religious traditions. We conclude this chapter with a look at Jesus's parables, especially that of the sower in Mark 4, to see how stories that are confusing, even for the disciples, are stories that help us realize the dangers of being insiders: the privilege of being an insider can make us complacent, intolerant, even wrong.

Chapter 2, on Mark 5–7, takes us to Jesus's rejection in Nazareth, a story that both Matthew and Luke rewrite, likely because they were uncomfortable with the idea that Jesus was incapable of performing miracles. We next look at the mission of the disciples in the light of the death of John the Baptizer, an "intercalated" or "sandwiched" story in which one helps to interpret the other. As Mark alerts us, the line between miracle and martyrdom, discipleship and death, is very thin. This chapter ends with the story of Jesus's debate with Pharisees over handwashing, ritual purity, and morality. Here we learn about the historical Pharisees, explore how ritual can bring meaning and order to life, and discuss how metaphors help us think in new ways about values and behavior.

Chapter 3 brings us to the Gospel's turning point, Mark 8–10, where the evangelist takes us from impenetrable parables and commands to keep news of miracles quiet to Jesus's stark announcement that he is going to suffer and die, and on the third day rise. We'll unpack Jesus's statement that some of his disciples will not taste death before they see the Kingdom come in power. Then we climb the mountain, traditionally identified as Mount Tabor, to witness Jesus's metamorphosis (Luke uses the term "transfiguration," but Mark really does use the term "metamorphosis"), where his divinity leaks through his humanity and where he appears with Moses and Elijah (9:2-13). We then look at one of, to my mind, Mark's most profound lines: the father of a demon-possessed boy who begs Jesus, *Help my unbelief* (9:24). We end this chapter with the third Passion prediction (10:32-34, 45) better to understand Jesus as the suffering servant, the martyr, and the ransom for many.

Chapter 4 begins the Passion Narrative with Jesus's entry into Jerusalem in Mark 11. We encounter one of the stories that my students resist: the cursing of the fig tree. Following is our discussion of the parable of the wicked tenants from Mark 12—which, like the story of the fig tree, I find disturbing. Accepting the allegory of the "Lord of the vineyard" as God, his murdered son as Jesus, and the tenants as the Jerusalem political establishment, we also look to the parable as an invitation to recognize, and then to repudiate, violence.

Chapter 5 concerns Mark 13, the "little apocalypse," where Jesus predicts the destruction of the Temple and then details, in highly symbolic language, the end of the world as we know it. His description includes the coming in glory and power of the Son of Humanity (often translated "Son of Man": the Greek is *anthrōpos*, whence "anthropology"), the title he uses as his self-designation. We'll see how this chapter both encourages and challenges, both assures and keeps us readers from becoming complacent.

Chapter 6, on Mark 14 and 15, focuses on two figures who continue both to fascinate and to disturb me and, perhaps, you. First, we meet the enigmatic Judas Iscariot, fated to betray Jesus. Mark's picture of Judas forces questions of predestination and personal responsibility, of the inexplicability of evil and of the limits of forgiveness. Second, we come to Mark's most enigmatic figure, the young man who flees, naked, from Gethsemane.

The conclusion brings us to Mark 16: its initial eight verses that describe the women's visit to the tomb, their encounter with a young man (who may be the streaker of Mark 14, or an angel, or both), and the women's flight in fear and silence. For some of the early followers of Jesus, Mark's initial ending—which I think is brilliant!—was insufficient. The so-called "longer" ending of Mark is where we find the commendation of taking up serpents and drinking poison. Given the Gospel's downplaying of miracles in favor of the suffering of Jesus, Mark likely would have been appalled at these additions.

I think Mark wanted people to read this Gospel, or, if they could not read (which would be most people in antiquity), to hear the text, again and again. Each time through, new mysteries and marvels, new revelations and reflections, appear. The text is inexhaustible in meaning.

CHAPTER 1

The Good News Begins

Mark 1–4

John and His Baptism

Mark's Gospel was not simply read from a scroll, page by page; more likely, the reader would explain the text passage by passage. Otherwise, the opening is like whiplash. First, we have the *Beginning of the Gospel of Jesus Messiah* with *Son of God* perhaps added. And immediately we get a quote that is a mash-up of verses from the prophets, a quote that is less about Jesus than it is about John the Baptizer. Mysteries abound: Who is this John? Why is he dunking people in the Jordan River? Why, if he promotes repentance, is Jesus coming to him—did Jesus sin?

Mark 1:2-3 reads:

> *Just as it is written in Isaiah the prophet, "Look, I send my messenger before your face, who will prepare your way. A voice crying in the desert, ['You (pl.)] prepare the way of the lord. Straight [you (pl.)] make his paths."*

Mark likes Isaiah (Isaiah is the only named prophet in the Gospel), but despite Mark's attribution, the citation combines Malachi 3:1 and Isaiah 40:3-4. Malachi 3:1 says, *See, I am sending my messenger to prepare the way before me.* I imagine Mark putting pen to papyrus and, with a smile, thinking, "I wonder if readers will know that I am quoting not just Isaiah but also Malachi?" Mark may be imagining even more.

The opening, "Look"—or "Behold"; I opted for "look" since I've yet to hear someone say to me, "AJ, behold"—prompts us to picture the storyteller pointing, and then the heads in the audience turning. At whom do we look? The "messenger" from God. The term is *angelos*, so not only do we look, we also hear: we hear an echo of that opening term *eu-angeliou*. First there is a good message, and now there is a messenger to begin its proclamation.

Mark immediately raises questions about the popular search for heavenly messengers in contemporary contexts. I wonder: Why look for angels with harps and haloes when the messages we need to hear may be from the friend who calls to ask how we are doing? We look for a word from God and so for good news in ancient texts, but we may also hear it coming from shelters or nonprofits or encampments of asylum seekers at the border. There are angels, good-news givers, all around, if we have ears to hear.

Next, audiences who know the initial line is from Malachi will likely also know that Malachi ends by predicting the coming of the prophet Elijah to announce the messianic age. Elijah, introduced in 1 Kings, never dies; rather, he is in bodily form, in heaven (via that sweet chariot that swung low), which means he can return at any time. In the Jewish tradition, Elijah attends every Passover seder (we open the door for him); he is sort of like a Jewish version of Santa Claus coming down the chimney. Santa delivers presents and gets milk and cookies (the reindeer get carrots); Elijah signals the promise of redemption and gets sweet wine. For Mark, John the Baptizer takes the role of Elijah, here to announce the arrival of the Messiah. In 9:13, after the Metamorphosis where Elijah appears, Jesus tells his disciples that *Elijah has come*. The reference to this returning Elijah is to John the Baptizer.

Making Mark's citation to Malachi even more meaningful: in the Septuagint, the basis of the church's Old Testament, Malachi is the last book. The Jewish canon (the Masoretic text) as developed in the Middle Ages tucks the Prophets in the middle and ends with

2 Chronicles. By alluding to Malachi, Mark again shows the continuity from the Scriptures of the Hellenistic Jewish community to the Gospel of Jesus.

Finally, for Mark, the "your" as in "before your face" and to "prepare your way" is Jesus. John the Baptizer is, for Mark, the messenger who comes before Jesus, both physically, to baptize him, and socially, to prepare anyone who will listen for his messianic message.

Understanding ancient texts as referring to something in the present is a not a misreading. The authors of some of the Dead Sea Scrolls saw their community as predicted by the ancient prophets as well. The meaning of a text will always outstrip what its author intended. New generations will ask new questions; new intertexts will provide additional insight into the original text. We continually pose to great literature questions that the authors may not have considered; sometimes we find new answers.

> **We continually pose to great literature questions that the authors may not have considered; sometimes we find new answers.**

Mark next sees something in Isaiah 40:2-3 that the author of those verses may not have seen. Mark finds new meaning, in effect, by redefining terms and changing the punctuation. Since technically punctuation hadn't yet been invented, such adaptation was easy to do.

Isaiah was writing to the covenant community in sixth-century BCE Babylon. The prophet's good news to them is that their exile is ending. King Cyrus of Persia (today's Iran) has conquered Babylon (today's Iraq) and is repatriating the Judeans taken into captivity. Politically, Cyrus needs allies on the Mediterranean; theologically, Cyrus is for Isaiah "God's anointed," "God's messiah," or "God's Christ" (Isaiah 45:1) who ends the exile. The community in Isaiah's time was out of place; for Mark's readers, whether in antiquity or today, there still may be a sense of dislocation. Part of the good news of Mark's Gospel is finding "home," as we'll see as we continue.

Now we come to punctuation. Isaiah wrote, were we to punctuate, *A voice crying, 'In the desert, prepare the way of the Lord'* (40:3). The prophet exhorts: go to the desert and build a highway from Babylon to Jerusalem, because you are going home. Isaiah calls for road construction. Mark moves the imagined comma and the imagined quotation mark: *A voice crying in the desert* (1:3), and that voice is the voice of the Baptizer dipping people into the Jordan.

Along with repurposing Malachi and Isaiah, Mark encodes additional hints about Jesus's mission. For example, "way," as in "prepare the way" in Greek is *hodos*, the origin of the English term "odometer," a mileage indicator. According to Acts 9:2 (see also 19:9, 23; 22:4; 24:14, 22), the early followers of Jesus were not called "Christians." They were known as the "followers of the way" (*hodos*). Isaiah spoke about building a way, a highway; Mark repurposes: the way being constructed is the way Jesus's disciples will follow.

This way is "of the Lord," and "Lord" in Greek is *kyrios*; the underlying Hebrew is *YHWH*. The pneumonic (to remember that the "Lord" translates *YHWH*) is that YHWH has four letters and is referred to as the "Tetragrammaton," a Greek word that, appropriately, means "four letters," so also "Lord" has four letters. But Mark imbues the term with additional meaning, for "Lord" (again, the problem with whether to capitalize) is the title Jesus's followers give him.

For Isaiah the "Lord" is YHWH; for Mark, this Lord is Jesus. Nowhere does the Gospel clearly designate Jesus as the divine "Lord"; thus, readers must determine for themselves, when someone identifies Jesus as *kyrios*, should we think "lord" with a lowercase "l" and the sense of "sir," or should we think "Lord" with an uppercase "L" and with the sense of "God incarnate."

Who is preparing this "way"? The imperative verbs are in the plural, as "Y'all" (I live in Nashville), or "yous" (I do recognize that "yous guys" is on Stanford's list of terms to avoid) do the preparation:

anyone who can hear Isaiah's voice or Mark's Gospel. It is the responsibility of "all y'all" to do the preparatory work.

Mark 1:4-8 describes this mysterious figure:

John, the one baptizing, appeared in the desert, and he was proclaiming a baptism of repentance regarding the forgiving of sins. And were coming out to him all the Judean region and the Jerusalemites, all, and they were being baptized by him in the Jordan River, confessing their sins. And John was clothed in camel hair, and a leather belt around his waist, and he was eating locusts and field honey. And he proclaimed, saying, "Is coming the one stronger than me, after me, of whom not am I worthy, bending, to loose the thong of his sandal. I baptized you by water, but he himself will baptize you in the Holy Spirit."

Then as now, location matters. The Greek term for "desert" or "wilderness" recollects Israel's forty-year sojourn before entering the Promised Land. The setting suggests the beginning of a new way of life, which is what Jesus will shortly proclaim when he states *The Kingdom of God has come near* (Mark 1:15). The setting also suggests a retreat from comfort. Mark is not talking about glamping. Mark is suggesting a reset: leave behind what makes us comfortable; open ourselves to new possibilities including, as did ancient Israel in the wilderness, a renewed sense of dependence on God. What needs to be left behind? What needs to be lifted up?

What needs to be confessed? The expression *baptism of repentance regarding the forgiving of sins* (1:4) needs unpacking. The ritual, which likely meant full-body immersion, is related to the *miqveh*, the Jewish bath for ritual purity, but it has a different function. Jewish washing, including the handwashing in Mark 7:1-20, concerned ritual purity and not sin. One immersed after contacting a corpse (e.g., preparing and burying a body), menstruation or ejaculation, childbirth, etc. Nothing to do with sin here. Just as Mark repurposes the words of the prophets, John repurposes the ritual.

We might think of John as promoting an ancient altar call, an invitation for people to repent and then rededicate themselves toward doing what God wants. Such repentance is needed, since as John puts it, someone stronger than he is coming, and this coming one will baptize not with water but in the Holy Spirit. John thereby suggests that the present, right now, is the time to repent. Repenting means fixing broken relationships and so doing one's best to restore community. Public testimony, and John's baptism is a public act, means that others present are responsible for keeping the repentant one on the right path.

> **Repenting means fixing broken relationships and so doing one's best to restore community.**

The first step in repentance is to confess one's sins. The next step is to make restitution where it is possible, and the related third is to turn from sin to righteousness. The Hebrew term for repentance, *teshuva*, literally means to "turn" as in turn away from the evil and toward the good. The Greek term in Mark 1:4, *metanoia*, also has the sense of changing one's thought patterns.

Many commentaries suggest that John is engaging in an anti-Temple protest by taking away the priests' monopoly on granting forgiveness. According to this reading, one need not go to the Temple or pay for a sacrifice; one only needed to go to John, whose penitence is cost-free. This view, while it has a cachet especially with people who are "spiritual but not religious" or who do not appreciate the communal aspects of religious affiliation, misunderstands Jewish practice and belief. God was, and is, always ready to forgive the repentant sinner. Sacrifice is not required to be in a right relation with God. Rather, John's baptism is a personal reset in light of eschatological urgency. So, too, a tent revival is not a replacement for regular church attendance; the two complement each other.

None of Jesus's followers, as far as we know, rejected Temple worship. Paul refers to it as one of the irrevocable gifts God gave to the Jews (Romans 9:4 mentions "worship" or "service" [Greek: *latreia*], which meant the worship in the Jerusalem Temple), and Acts shows the followers, including Paul, not only worshipping in the Temple but also sacrificing there (see Acts 21:26). Since the Temple worked on a sliding scale, people who wished to make an offering, as do Mary and Joseph in Luke 2:24, were able to do so regardless of economic status. Comparable would be passing a collection plate on a Sunday morning in church: people give what they can, and if they cannot give anything, they are still welcome.

As for John, many people at the time regarded him as a prophet. While what we call "classical prophecy" and hence biblical prophetic texts end with Malachi, our first-century historian Josephus speaks of Essenes as having prophetic abilities. He mentions "sign prophets" such as Theudas and "the Egyptian," a prophet named Jesus the son of Ananias, and another prophet named Menahem who both predicted the rule of Herod the Great and exhorted Herod to behave in a just manner. Josephus even attributes prophetic abilities to himself. John would have registered to some Jews as a prophet, as did Jesus.

When I first heard that John wore a "camel-hair coat," I thought of high-end shopping. Today's (expensive) camel-hair coats are made from the hair of the bactrian camel (two humps), with the industry centered in Mongolia and surrounding regions, but the dromedary (one hump) is native to the Middle East. John likely wore what Zechariah 13:4 calls a "hairy mantle" (which, contrary to my initial impression, has nothing to do with the shelf over the fireplace, and just as well), a garment marking an individual as a prophet.

As for his diet, locusts combined with wild honey suggests John is living off the land. On the other hand, the Greek term for "locust" sounds like the term for "honey cake." Mark may be hinting at manna, the "bread from heaven" ancient Israel ate in the wilderness (Exodus 16:31; Numbers 11:8; popular etymology proposes that "manna" comes from the Hebrew *man hu*, meaning "What is that?"). Other explanations strike me as less likely, for example, that locusts are related to the plagues in Egypt or that honey concerned promised land, flowing with "milk and honey" (e.g., Exodus 3:8). It is our task, or gift, as readers to determine what, and when, symbolism is in play or which readings we find palatable.

John's message is, like his setting, one of anticipation. Some in John's original audience, already disciples, would understand "baptism in the Holy Spirit" in terms of spiritual gifts, such as speaking in tongues (see Acts 2; 10; 19; 1 Corinthians 12–14) or healing. We might also think about the Holy Spirit as "possessing" people, but in a good way. If we are possessed by the Holy Spirit, the Spirit then works in and through us. Just as Satan can possess people, so can the Spirit.

The Baptism of Jesus

Mark's opening scene ends with Jesus's baptism. In Matthew's version, John insists that Jesus, being the greater of the two, baptize him, and Jesus responds that John should perform the ritual for the sake of "righteousness" (one of Matthew's favorite terms). In Luke's Gospel, John and Jesus are cousins, and even when they are *in utero*, John acknowledges Jesus's superiority (1:41). In the Fourth Gospel, John never baptizes Jesus (there's a baptism scene in John 1, but no baptism). Mark, who has had John announce his subordinate status vis-à-vis Jesus, offers the following unembellished account in 1:9-11:

> And it was in those days, came Jesus from Nazareth of Galilee, and he was baptized in the Jordan by John. And immediately, coming up out of the water, he saw splitting the heavens, and the Spirit as a dove coming down to him. And a voice came out of the heavens, 'You are my Son, the beloved, with you I am well pleased.'

John is baptizing for the remission of sin, and John baptizes Jesus. The logical conclusion is that Jesus had sinned. The Epistle to the Hebrews (which, I find myself consistently noting, Jews generally don't read since it is not the Jewish canon) states that Jesus *in every respect has been tested (or tempted, or brought to trial) as we are, yet without sin* (Hebrews 4:15). We can, following this epistle as well as later church teaching, regard Jesus as sinless, or we can, in Mark's account, see him as knowing what it is like to sin, to repent, and to be forgiven.

There is a third option beyond the "he sinned" and "he did not sin" to explain Jesus's baptism. Jewish life then, and now, is communitarian. On the Day of Atonement (Yom Kippur), we pray: "forgive *us*...." The "*Our* Father" (note that "our"!) prayer includes the verse, "Forgive *us our*" debts, sins, trespasses—all are viable readings. Atoning in the plural, as being a member of a community means that one person's sin impacts the many. Even if we were not personally responsible for committing a particular sin, we still atone as a community. By accepting John's baptism, Jesus can be seen as accepting his role as a part of the human community. He also sets an example for his followers.

According to Mark, the heavens ripped or split apart (the Greek verb is *schidzō*, whence "schism"). The same term appears in Mark 15:38 to describe the tearing of the Temple veil. The symbolism of the veil does not, contrary to some claims, indicate that forgiveness is now available, outside the Temple, to Gentiles, people who were ritually impure (e.g., suffering from vaginal hemorrhages or leprosy), or the poor. The Temple could not and did not restrict either forgiveness or salvation. Nor was there a barrier between humanity and divinity that needed to be broken. The opening of the heavens at the beginning of Mark's Gospel and the voice that descends is known in Hebrew as a *Bat Qol*, the "daughter of the voice." This voice speaks in rabbinic literature as well. The opening of the heavens here, repeated at the cross, tells us that Jesus was never alone, even though he cried out, "My God, my God, why have you forsaken me" (Mark 15:34, quoting Psalm 22:1). God has ripped the heavens, as Jews rip a garment when in mourning. God is present, even when we most acutely feel the absence.

The dove can recall the dove Noah sent to determine if it were safe to leave the ark (Genesis 8:8-12), or gentleness (Psalm 74:19), or a variety of other images that "dove" or, for that matter, "pigeon," would evoke. It seems to me historically plausible that as Jesus rose from the water, he saw a dove and interpreted it as a divine message. This approach means being open to the natural world. It means heavenly signs can be as ordinary as a pigeon strutting on the sidewalk. It means that all signs require interpretation.

This baptism engages our senses: the touch of John's hands, the wet of the water on the skin, the vision of the dove, the hearing of the voice. For Mark, the voice speaks directly to Jesus; it is personal, even intimate: *You are my son, the beloved; with you I am well pleased* (1:11). The voice confirms Jesus's mission. Mark here also unites Jesus with the audience of the Gospel: *we* like Jesus hear the voice from heaven. *We* know what the other people coming to John that day do not.

This voice from heaven can be taken as announcing an adoption; for Mark, Jesus's role as God's anointed comes not at conception or birth; it comes when Jesus submits to John's baptism. The voice is also a mash-up of Psalm 2:7 LXX (a royal psalm depicting God telling the Davidic king, *My son you are; I today have begotten you*), Isaiah 42:1 (one of the so-called "servant songs," which reads, *Here is my servant [or slave], I support him, my chosen [in whom] is pleased my soul; I give my spirit upon him; justice to the nations he will bring forth*) and perhaps Genesis 22:2 (God's command to Abraham to sacrifice Isaac, *the son whom you love*). Again, Mark repurposes the words of the ancient prophets. These early texts can be seen, retrospectively, as pointing to Jesus, but they will always have additional meanings, whether in their own historical contexts, or as read by (non-messianic) Jews, or as read by anyone who sees the texts as still having something to say. Anyone can be a beloved child, a suffering servant, a seeker of justice.

> **We contact the people with whom we need to**
> **reconcile; we apologize for the harmful comment**
> **or the failure to send a greeting or a get-well wish;**
> **we live as if what we do matters. And it does.**

Mark 1:10, the description of how Jesus came up from the water and the Spirit descended upon him, offers the first use of *kai euthus*, the Greek expression translated as "and immediately." It is the first of forty-two uses in Mark. The Gospel has a sense of urgency: repent *now*, decide *now*, act *now*. After two thousand years-plus, the idea of the imminent in-breaking of the kingdom of God may seem exaggerated. It should not. It is never too late; it is always the right time to repent. As Rabbi Eliezer says in *Pirke Avot* 2:10 (*Ethics of the Fathers*, a tractate in the Mishnah), "repent (Hebrew: *shuv*, as in *teshuvah*) one day before your death." We contact the people with whom we need to reconcile; we apologize for the harmful comment or the failure to send a greeting or a get-well wish; we live as if what we do *matters*. And it does.

Into the Wilderness

Mark's first chapter then takes us into the wilderness, where "and immediately" the Spirit casts Jesus (1:12) and where he spends forty days, like ancient Israel who spent forty years in the wilderness (Numbers 32:13). The reference also reminds us of Elijah's forty-day journey to Mount Horeb, another name for Mount Sinai (1 Kings 19:8). Jesus, like Moses and Elijah is tested. All prophets are, since is it easier to go with the status quo than to fight for justice. We are tempted by all sorts of distractions, as we'll see when we get to the parable of the sower in Mark 4. Here in the first chapter, Mark depicts Jesus as tested, or tempted, by Satan. Not only does Jesus overcome the temptation, but he also shows his followers that Satan can be defeated, that whatever keeps us from being on the right path can be dislodged.

When Herod Antipas arrests John, Jesus begins his public message. Mark makes note of the timing. Jesus is not in competition with John. Moreover, in narrative context, Jesus's proclamation of the "gospel" is juxtaposed to John's arrest. The connection is not arbitrary; rather, it anticipates Jesus's own arrest and execution.

Mark tells us that Jesus came *proclaiming the good news of God* (1:14). His message is simple: *Fulfilled is the time and has come near the Kingdom of God; repent and trust in the good news* (1:15). These are Jesus's first words in the Gospel. The term for "time" Mark uses here, *kairos*, can be distinguished from clock time (*chronos*). Time can seem dreadfully slow ("will this lecture ever end?") and incredibly fast ("that vacation seemed over before it started"). *Kairos* time is on God's watch; it is not a minute-to-minute concern but a recognition that something special is happening. When I look at my watch, I can do more than determine how much time I have to finish a project. I can think about God's time: what should I have done that I have failed to do? What can I do to do make every moment meaningful?

With its first fifteen verses, Mark sets the agenda for the good news to come. We will learn: what it means to be both Son of God and fully human; how what Christians will come to call the "Old Testament" is understood in light of the life and death of Jesus; how Jesus should be understood within a specific time and place; how the Holy Spirit can possess Jesus, or anyone else, with a sense of divine commission and the strength to carry it out; how nature can be revelatory; how prophets face temptation and more but can overcome all stumbling blocks; that the proclamation of the in-breaking of the kingdom of God should prompt repentance; and so much more.

More in Mark 1

In Mark 1:16, Jesus calls *Simon and Andrew the brother of Simon*. Underlying the call is Jeremiah 16:16, where God announces, *I am now sending for many fishermen. . . . [A]nd immediately* (1:18) Simon (later renamed Peter, so in chapter 1, again Mark tells the audience more than the other people in the Gospel know!) and Andrew leave their nets and follow Jesus. The brothers James (actually, the Greek reads "Jacob") and John follow suit (1:19), as they leave their father and follow Jesus.

The rest of Mark 1 presents Jesus as teaching in the Capernaum synagogue (1:21-22), when he exorcises a man possessed by an unclean spirit and so demonstrates his powers over Satan (1:23-27). We learn of the spread of Jesus's reputation as an exorcist (1:28), and we see him entering the home of Peter and Andrew where he heals many, including Peter's mother-in-law who is suffering from a fever (1:29-34). Peter's mother-in-law (I do wish we had a name for her) then rises to serve [Greek *diakoneō*, whence "deacon"] Jesus and, perhaps (the manuscripts disagree) the disciples as well. This service makes her Mark's first "deacon." We find Jesus teaching and exorcising in Galilee (1:35-39) and cleansing a man from leprosy (1:40-45). You may want to spend more time with all these stories in Mark 1. The swiftness, the immediacy, of the narrative can be exhausting, or exhilarating. I get the impression of Jesus as doing everything, from receiving his affirmation at the baptism to fighting cosmic battles with Satan, from proclaiming the good news of the Kingdom to manifesting that good news in providing medical care.

The chapter also raises questions: What do these events suggest to you about the "good news"? About the type of "messiah" Jesus is? About what the world needs, then and now?

The Call of the Tax Collector (Mark 2:14-17)

For Mark 2, we follow Jesus next to the call of Levi the tax collector in 2:13-17 and so matters of table fellowship, how one is judged by the company one keeps, and how Jesus distinguishes between the righteous and sinners.

Here is Mark 2:14-17, the calling not of the righteous (are we among the righteous?) but the sinners (or are we among the sinners?):

And walking along, he saw Levi, the [son] of Alphaeus, sitting at the toll booth, and he says to him, "Follow me." And rising, he followed him.

And it happens, when he was reclining, in his house, and many tax collectors and sinners were reclining with Jesus, and with his disciples, for there were many, and they were following him.

And the scribes of the Pharisees, seeing that he eats with the sinners and the tax collectors, were saying to his disciples that "with the tax collectors and sinners he eats."

And hearing, Jesus says to them, that "not need do they have, the strong, of a physician, but the ones having sickness. Nor have I come to call righteous, but sinners."

When I was a child, my mother warned me, "Don't hang out with the guys who smoke dope" or "Don't hang out with the girls who shoplift." We all knew who "they" were, and we all knew why association could be a problem: We are known by the company we keep; birds of a feather flock together; lie down with dogs and wake up with fleas.

Tax collectors, *in antiquity*, had a bad reputation (heaven forbid I would say something negative about IRS agents). Tax collectors made their money by topping off for personal gain taxes due to Rome or its local representatives; some held monopolies on certain products, such as salt. Luke 3:12-13 describes tax collectors asking John the Baptizer what they should do, and John replies, *No more than the amount assigned to you collect* [lit. *accomplish*]. Matthew 11:19 connects tax collectors and sinners with gluttons and drunkards and makes all four friends of Jesus. Tax collectors and sinners are not just people trying to make a living; they are the ancient versions of loan sharks and drug dealers, pimps and traitors. Gluttons and drunkards, who have more than enough to eat and drink, are the ancient versions of those who engage in conspicuous consumption.

A number of Christian commentators see these tax collectors and their friends as "outcast" because they associate with Gentiles and are therefore supposedly ritually impure. Again, the claim misunderstands Jewish practice and belief. The Jerusalem Temple was a "house of prayer for all people" since Gentiles were welcomed into the outer court. Synagogues welcomed Gentiles as Godfearers. The Pharisees are not concerned about ritual impurity in Mark 2; they are curious as to why Jesus associates with people who harm the community. These tax collectors and their friends are neither "outcast" nor, given their finances, economically "marginal." To the contrary, they left the community, and its values, on their own two feet.

Jesus, diagnosing social sin—gluttony, selfishness, and sanctimoniousness—as a type of disease, explains that he is a physician who makes house calls. I find this medical metaphor helpful. Rather than use social shame to treat such behaviors or habits, it might be better to think about treating diseases. Greed prompts more greed, so what can be done to break the system? Desire for power prompts the desire for more power, so what can be done to stop the drive? Bringing sinners to repentance is more likely to occur with care than with condemnation. Helping people to learn to help others is a better way of helping them to help themselves out of the practices of sin and into the practices of righteousness.

> **Bringing sinners to repentance is more likely to occur with care than with condemnation.**

The early followers of Jesus did not, for the most part, continue Jesus's practice of dining with tax collectors and sinners. In 1 Corinthians 5:9-11, Paul instructs, *I wrote to you in my letter not to associate with sexually immoral persons... or robbers, or greedy, or one who is an idolater, reviler, drunkard, or robber. Do not even eat with such a person.* Paul sounds like my mother. As a teenager, I would have put myself in social danger by associating with the "druggies" and the shoplifters. However, now, as an adult, I teach when I can at Riverbend Maximum Security Institution in Nashville, where I work with people who have committed crimes (I'd eat with them, if visitors were allowed to bring in food). Such association is frequently healing for both my insider students and for me.

It's no wonder that *the scribes of the Pharisees* (2:16) questioned the disciples about Jesus's dining habits. Levi is hosting a banquet—we know it is a banquet both because of the *many tax collectors and sinners* present and because the guests are *reclining* (2:15). This is the A-list for the socially malignant.

The scribes have no idea that Jesus told these people to repent; nor apparently do the disciples, since Jesus has to provide the answer. He sees sin as a disease, and he is the physician who has the skill to facilitate healing.

In this scene, one of many in the Gospel, Mark emphasizes eating and drinking: *he eats with the sinners and the tax collectors . . . with the tax collectors and sinners, he eats* (2:16). Commensality, eating with others, is a hallmark of Jesus's ministry. To break bread with people is to suggest a relationship with them. More, eating and drinking remind us of the eschatological banquet in which *will make the Lord of Hosts for all the peoples on this mountain a banquet of rich food, a banquet of well-aged wine* (Isaiah 25:6). The Greek translation (LXX) even says they *will drink joy!* Meeting people at table, Jesus provides a foretaste of the Messianic banquet even as he facilitates repentance. I would feel better had Mark stated that everyone at the table repented and returned whatever they had extorted. Perhaps they did. Perhaps they may. Sometimes treatment requires several house calls.

Our tax collector Levi may have experienced such healing. Mark introduces him as seated at his toll booth, and on Jesus's command, he gets up and leaves. He resembles Peter and Andrew, James and John, who *immediately left their nets* to follow Jesus (1:16-20).

Levi, too, may have axed his day job, but rather than leave everything behind, he repurposes what he has.

According to Matthew 10:3, among the disciples was a "Matthew the tax collector." This Matthew appears to be the same fellow as the Levi we meet here in Mark (also in Luke 5:27). In 3:17-18, Mark lists the twelve disciples, but no Levi appears in the list and no tax collector. There is a "James, son of Alphaeus." Levi's brother? Perhaps Mark's Levi had second thoughts about this kingdom of God project. Mark asks us to speculate on his fate and so to finish his story.

From Feasting to Fasting

The scene now shifts from feasting to fasting (2:18-22). Fasting can be individual; for example, David fasts while the son conceived in adultery with Bathsheba is dying (2 Samuel 12:16). In Luke 18:12, a Pharisee in a parable mentions that he fasts twice a week and thus he exemplifies personal piety and self-discipline.

More often, fasting is communal. Zechariah 7:3-5 mentions a fast connected with the destruction of the Jerusalem Temple (587 BCE); Jews maintain this fast day, on the ninth of the month of Av (Hebrew: *Tisha b'Av*). For the Day of Atonement, Yom Kippur, Jews fast for twenty-five hours starting at sundown and going to the next sundown. Being together in the synagogue during the day and into the evening is sustaining. Some Christians fast, whether for personal discipline, as a Lenten sacrifice, and/or in solidarity with those suffering food insecurity, or on days such as Ash Wednesday and Good Friday.

The disciples of the Baptizer and the disciples of the Pharisees fasted, for personal discipline, as a mark of piety, and as a form of communal repentance. Jesus explains that his disciples do not fast, because he is the *bridegroom* and one cannot fast at a wedding (Mark 2:19). To be with Jesus, who heals bodies of disease and who brings the message of repentance to sinners, is a time to celebrate, to feast and not fast. It is like being at a wedding, where new relationships are created.

Others may have seen the *lack* of fasting by Jesus's disciples as promoting gluttony or self-indulgence. As with Jesus's dining with sinners, such a judgment is a misreading. Such misunderstanding prompts the questions: What do we do in communal or personal worship that could be misunderstood? It ist often salutary to invite people from different traditions to a worship service and then ask how they interpreted the art, the rituals, the words, and the music. If to be with Jesus is to have the joy one would have at a wedding, is that joy found in worship? If Jesus can welcome people who have walked out of the community for the sake of their own appetites or bank accounts, what are his followers doing to help them return?

In the Grainfield

Misunderstanding of practices promoted by Jesus or practiced by his followers continues into the final scene in Mark 2. Here we find the disciples, plucking heads of grain on the Sabbath, rubbing the grain between their fingers to get off the husk, and then eating the grain. Pharisees question why they are violating the Sabbath by reaping, a form of work.

It is unclear to me why Pharisees, on the Sabbath, would be hanging out in grainfields. I wonder if Mark invented the scene, given that Mark is no fan of the Pharisees. Jesus responds by asking the Pharisees if they had never read about how David, when he and his friends were starving, ate bread reserved for the priests. In fact, they never did read this, since Jesus misquotes the text (you can check this for yourselves): 1 Samuel 21:1-6 depicts David alone; he is not starving; we never see him eat the bread. More, Jesus names the priest in the temple as Abiathar when his name was Ahimelech.

Did the Pharisees read this story? No. Does their silence indicate not only that Jesus has bested them in the debate but also that they did not know their own texts? Could be. I do sometimes invent Bible verses when I get the impression that students in a seminar have not done the reading. I think Mark has Jesus deliberately misquote the story in 1 Samuel 21 to show the lack of knowledge on the part of the Pharisees. And so Mark 2 raises the question of how well we know the texts we consider to be sacred.

At the chapter's end, Jesus announces that the Sabbath is for people, not people for the Sabbath (Mark 2:27). Jewish sources agree. The Babylonian Talmud, Yoma 85b makes the same point. While most people agree that a day of rest is a good idea, there is little agreement on what "rest" or "do not work" means. Jesus's disciples will need to determine for themselves how to celebrate the day of rest: what must be done, what should never be done, what is negotiable, and what may have changed over time.

The Parable of the Sower (Mark 4)

For Mark 4, we look at the parable of the sower, what it might have meant for Jesus's or Mark's original audiences, and what it might mean for us. To anticipate: here is one of several passages that, when I went to Riverbend to teach a course on Mark, I thought I knew what it meant. When I left, I had another understanding.

This is the parable of the sower, or the parable of the different soils, Mark 4:3-9:

Listen! Look! Went out the sower to sow.

And it happened when he was sowing, on the one hand, some fell by the road, and came the birds, and they ate it.

And other fell upon the rocky way, where not did it have much earth, and immediately it rose up on account of its not having depth of ground. And when rose the sun, it was scorched, even on account of its not having a root, it withered.

And other fell into the thorns, and rose up the thorns and choked it, and fruit not did it give.

But other fell into the good earth, and it was giving fruit, rising up and increasing and bearing one thirty, and one sixty, and one one hundred.

And he was saying, the one having ears to hear, hear!

Look! Listen! Mark's Jesus is addressing not only the crowds on the shore, he is also addressing readers then and now. Jesus asks us to develop a mental picture of this strange sower with his even stranger crop. People then and now may have thought of the sower as Jesus, spreading his word as the sower spreads his seeds, indiscriminately, to any who will listen.

But what kind of sower is this? Commentators sometimes talk about "broadcast" agriculture, where sowers toss seed indiscriminately. The problem here is that grain is a commodity, and farmers tend not to be cavalier about where they toss it. More, seed is generally sown on plowed ground. To toss seed onto soil that lacks depth or has thorns is weird, and wasteful. As one of my students, president of his school's chapter of Future Farmers of America, noted, "Jesus was a carpenter, not an agricultural worker."

Then again, this is a parable. Because we readers trust Jesus, we trust that whatever he says has a decipherable message. We also know from cross-cultural fairy tales and folktales that this parable uses a familiar form of storytelling: two or three negatives, and then a hyperbolic positive: two ugly stepsisters and the gorgeous Cinderella, for example, or two pigs who know nothing about construction and one with a degree in engineering. Jesus teases us by describing three negatives and a very positive fourth result.

The rest of the Gospel offers clues for interpreting the parable. For example, the seed that *fell by the road, and came the birds, and they ate it* (Mark 4:4) is seed that never took root. That image correlates to those who oppose Jesus, preeminent of whom are the Pharisees, Mark's stock villains. The seed that *fell upon the rocky way, where not did it have much earth, and...withered* (4:5) can refer to people who have no depth to their attachment to the gospel. They come for the healing or the exorcism, look like they are going to become followers, and then give up. What happened, for example, to those five thousand whom Jesus fed? Where were they when he was put on public trial in Jerusalem? Were the disciples, last seen fleeing from Gethsemane, the seed that withered, or do they have a chance at growth? The seeds that are choked by thorns are followers pulled away from discipleship by other demands—familial, political, economic, whatever. I think here of the would-be disciple in Mark 10:17-22 who was unable to sell all he had and give to the poor. He was choked by his stuff.

Finally, the seed that lands in *the good earth* (4:8) and produces a magnificent yield, that seed can represent the faithful followers. Intertextual echoes help us here as well. According to Genesis 26:12, *Isaac sowed seed…and in the same year reaped a hundred-fold. The* LORD *blessed him.* The magnificent yield is possible, with divine help.

The parable did not seem to me initially incomprehensible. I took it to mean that regarding Mark's good news—repent and believe that the Kingdom is at hand—some people never get it; some get it and then give up; some get it and then get distracted; and some stay the course. Most of my students see themselves as the seed that created the magnificent yield. That reading makes sense to me—we all want to think of ourselves as staying the course, and as being righteous, and as being successful.

But Mark tells me that I'm too self-confident in what I think I know (thanks, Mark). In Mark 4:10, some unknown and perhaps potential disciples ask Jesus in private about the parables. Jesus tells them—note, not the disciples, but those others, and perhaps us readers—*to you the mystery has been given of the Kingdom of God, but to those, the ones outside, in parables all things occur* (4:11).

Jesus is saying that I need to rethink my (simplistic?) interpretation. He then quotes Isaiah 6:9-10: *So that seeing, they may see and not know, and hearing they may hear and not understand, lest they turn, and it be forgiven to them.* Not helpful, Jesus. Here Matthew agrees with me (or less anachronistically, I agree with Matthew), since Matthew 13:13 copies the same quote from Mark but changes *so that* to *because* and eliminates *lest they turn, and it be forgiven to them.* Mark has Jesus teaching to condemn; Matthew softens the message.

It looks like the outsiders are doomed and the insiders will have both understanding and perseverance. I get the initial impression that Jesus is deliberately withholding comprehensible teachings from a huge swath of people. But again, I'm wrong. The insiders don't understand either. Jesus then says to his questioners, *Not do you know this parable? And how all the parables will you know?* (Mark 4:13). The insiders don't get it. They may never. Bear with me: when we take time with this very confusing section, clarity begins to emerge.

Having unsettled everyone, which is not a bad pedagogical move, Jesus now explains. It turns out that the sower may be Jesus, but not necessarily. The sower can be anyone who proclaims the gospel. Mark 4:14 states, *The one sowing sows the word.* While my initial impression was that the seed represents individuals who hear the gospel but react differently, in the allegorical explanation, the seed is not the listener but the "word" itself, that is, the good news of the Kingdom and of its Messiah.

The images are collapsing in on themselves. They disorient, and that's a very good thing in theological discussion. Mark 4 keeps us from being complacent, from being sure that we have all the right answers, from being too self-confident and from feeling secure that insider status (church membership, academic credentials, whatever) is a place of privilege.

Jesus's explanation continues, and I realized I've missed more and more. The allegory continues to unsettle. For example, the seed that landed by the road turns out to have been picked up by Satan. But then Satan takes the word (4:15)? The Word? How does that work? I'm starting to get a headache. I tried to make a chart of what represents what, but that didn't work. The rocky ground relates to those who fail to persevere because of *tribulation or persecution* (4:17); they are not the seed; they are the plant, but okay, this one I've got. Phew. Now the allegory shifts again, *for the others are the ones into the thorns are sown; these are the ones who hear the word* (4:18). Wait—so the seed is not the Word? The seed is the individual who lands among the thorns. They are choked by the *cares of the ages and the deceit of money* (4:19). Okay, back on track. And the seeds on the good earth are those who are faithful disciples (4:20). Mark makes me read, and reread, and then I run to friends to process, and then we together read again. Mark makes me aware of my own ignorance about salvation. Mark prevents me from judging others because I do not know what type of seed, or ground, they represent. Mark encourages me to figure out what has gone wrong: Have I been distracted, or have I been placed in a situation that does not yield itself to moral consideration or spiritual growth? And more.

Mark's parable-plus-allegory also raises the question: How do we become the good seed if we cannot control where we land?

> **Don't worry about the many who do not receive the message today, suggests Jesus. You can't do anything about the soil. Rather, rejoice in those who do receive your message.**

Without the confusing allegorical explanation, here's another message I initially took from the parable. Jesus tells his disciples that they are to proclaim the kingdom of God and by exorcising demons show that Satan was losing his grip (Mark 3:14-15). The disciples will scatter the seed of the good news to anyone who will listen. But as Jesus experienced opposition, so the disciples need to be prepared for rejection. Only a few people will respond positively and consistently to the call, but those few make all the difference. Don't worry about the many who do not receive the message today, suggests Jesus.

You can't do anything about the soil. Rather, rejoice in those who do receive your message.

And then I went to Riverbend. I suggested that Jesus is comforting the disciples over the anticipated rejection of this messianic proclamation. The job of the missionary is to spread the seed wherever; whether people receive it or not is up to God. Some people will listen; most will not, because soil does not change.

One of my insider students challenged me, and here I am paraphrasing because I did not write down his words. "I was the soil choked by thorns," he said. "I had no time for the gospel because other things were more important: power, prestige, money. Since being incarcerated and being around other men who had the same experiences as I did but who turned to Jesus, I've learned, how, with help, to clear away the thorns. Barren soil can be treated with fertilizer; rocks can be dug out, and thorns can be cleared. Seeds, when they are tended, can yield enormous growth."

More—and here it helps to know something about gardening (not my strong suit—on my knees in the dirt with the bugs and the worms, and I'd break a nail), that insider student insisted that even the seeds that are choked or eaten by birds will eventually return to and so replenish the soil. Nothing will go to waste. It may take longer for some of those seeds to germinate, but eventually they all can contribute to a good harvest.

> **You can determine for yourself if you are seed or soil, if you fully understand the parable or if you remain confused but intrigued. The parable, when it does the work of parables, will continue to provoke, to comfort, and to caution.**

He may be right. While academics will continue to discuss whether the allegorical explanation comes from Jesus, early interpreters, or Mark the evangelist, or whether the focus of the parable is the sower, the seed, or the soil, multiple messages may take root and yield a hundredfold. You can determine for yourself if you are seed or soil, if you fully understand the parable or if you remain confused but intrigued. The parable, when it does the work of parables, will continue to provoke, to comfort, and to caution.

CHAPTER 2

Restoring Purity
and Wholeness

Mark 5-7

Mark 4 ends with the stilling of the storm, and, following that, the disciples wondering about Jesus, *Who therefore is this, that even the wind and the sea obey him?* (4:41). For Mark's readers, if not for the Twelve, the answer is obvious: This is the Son of God. Mark's next three chapters, 5–7, develop this interest in Christology by showing Jesus defeating a legion, an army cohort of demons (Mark 5:1-20); conquering illness by restoring a hemorrhaging woman to a state of ritual purity; and conquering death by raising a twelve-year-old girl from the dead (5:21-43). The disciples, bless their hearts (as we say in the South), still don't understand who he is.

Mark 6, which, given these magnificent miracles, should have begun with a celebration of Jesus's messianic identity, instead shows how most of the people in his hometown failed to honor him. Amazed at the unbelief in Nazareth (speaking of seed sown on infertile soil), he begins his tour of the villages of lower Galilee. Now he also sends out the Twelve, two by two, on their own mission, and Mark 6:7-13 and 30 provides their instructions. Our focus text for this chapter is the next scene, Mark 6:14-29, the death of John the Baptizer, and the only narrative in Mark's Gospel that doesn't speak about Jesus. Here we see motifs that easily, and sadly, are no less prevalent now: corruption of those in power, illegal incarceration and capital punishment, misogyny, even the abuse of children. Following John's death, Mark 6 returns to Jesus: the feeding of the five thousand (6:31-44), his walking on water, and then another general healing (6:45-56).

Had Mark's first five chapters been insufficient for answering the question of who Jesus is, chapter 6 is abundantly clear. He is God Incarnate. No one else walks on water; no one else provides food for Israel in the wilderness. The disciples remain clueless. And yet, while this divine-human being can walk on water, there is nothing he can do in his hometown, save for a few healings, because of the people's unbelief. This divine-human can raise the dead, but he himself will die.

The disciples, too, participate in this paradox. They can exorcise demons, but they cannot convince human beings to listen to them. They are the advance guard to proclaim the good news of Jesus the Christ, Jesus the Messiah, but their fate will more likely be martyrdom than majesty. By sandwiching the story of the death of the Baptizer between the commission of the Twelve and their report back—this sandwiching is a literary technique called "intercalation," in which the bread (the disciples' mission) and the filling (the death of John) interpret each other—Mark warns: suffering will be more prominent than miracles, most of your seeds will not reach the harvest, but suffering and death are not the end of the story.

We end this chapter with Mark 7:1-20, Jesus's debate with the Pharisees concerning what creates uncleanness. This is one of the Gospel's most misunderstood narratives, since, in the Western popular imagination, such matters as the ritual washing of hands or dietary regulations can at first glance seem superstitious or silly. When we get the history right, we see that in fact Jesus and the Pharisees would have agreed on the basics; they disagreed on the particulars. I admit to agreement with the Pharisees on part of the argument and to agreement with Jesus on another part.

Missionary Practice (Mark 6:7-13, 30)

And summoning the Twelve, he began to send, two by two, and he was giving to them all authority over the unclean spirits.

And he commanded them that they should not take for (the) road except one staff; no bread, no bag, and no in the belt bronze [i.e., money]. But, wearing sandals, and not should they take two tunics.

And he was saying to them, "Wherever you might enter into a house, there remain until when you might go out from there. And whichever a place not having received you, neither having listened to you, when you are going out from there, shake off the dust beneath your feet in witness to them."

And, going out, they proclaimed that they might repent. And many demons they were casting out, and they were anointing with oil many sick people, and they were healing....

And came together the apostles to Jesus and they announced to him all that they had done and what they had taught.

No one said that being a disciple would be easy. The intercalation of the mission of the Twelve with the death of John tells the reader, but not the disciples, that their work could lead to death. The disciples, still wondering over the miracles they had witnessed, feel empowered. They do not yet know that Jesus will die or that their fate also may be one of humiliation and death.

And summoning the Twelve, he began to send, two by two (6:7). The first commission is to travel with a buddy. Mark does not explain the two-by-two approach (which reminds me of Noah's ark, where the animals went by twosies, twosies), but the instruction makes sense. First, the companion makes one less vulnerable to assault; That first fellow we meet in the parable of the good Samaritan, going down the Jerusalem to Jericho road, might have been spared attack had he an associate with him. Second, should the mission prove unfruitful, having a companion can help with the disappointment.

29

Third, the companion helps in terms of pulling away the thorns and providing necessary fertilizer: when our confidence flags or our body tell us that we cannot go any farther, that companion can carry us, spiritually and even physically. Some commentators suggest that two are needed because according to Deuteronomy 19:15 (also 17:6), two witnesses are needed for legal testimony; since the concern here is missional rather than judicial, and since the two would hardly be independent witnesses, this reading strikes me as unconvincing. Finally, mission can be a very lonely undertaking; even Jesus feels abandoned by God at times. Having a companion eases the loneliness.

The buddy model also reminds me of my friends in AA ("friends of Bill") who are sponsors of other members and who have their own sponsors. My friends maintain strict confidence in terms of identifying either their sponsors or the people whom they sponsor, but they do tell me stories of what words worked, of how knowing there was someone to call, even at 3 a.m., saved them. Friends are accountable to each other. When the system works, the two-by-two mission helps create trust, the incentive to go that extra mile, the ability to deal with those birds and those thorns.

We readers know that Judas will betray Jesus, since Mark 3:19, in listing the Twelve, speaks of *Judas Iscariot, who even betrayed* Jesus. But the Twelve in Mark 6 do not have this information. I wonder how the disciple who was paired with Judas Iscariot felt when Jesus was arrested. Did he think he had failed in that he could not keep Judas on the right path? Second guessing in such cases does not help; it only leads to greater feelings of either helplessness or guilt. Sponsors in AA encounter members who fail, some repeatedly. As individuals and as organizations (AA meetings, churches, civic groups), we cannot save everyone or, to go back to the parable, not all seed takes root the first time; but we continue the programs.

Jesus first gives the Twelve *all authority over the unclean spirits* (6:7). They had already seen him perform exorcisms; they had heard that the Strong Man (Satan) had been bound and his vessels plundered (Mark 3:27). They had this one. So, a final note on AA. One of my friends in AA described his alcoholism as a type of possession, as if the drink had control over him. Joining AA was his way of exorcising that demon. It can be done, one demon at a time, with the right sponsorship. Eventually, one might even become one's own exorcist. Intervention helps. Looking in the mirror and being honest helps. Having a support system helps.

Then comes instruction on what to bring. Packing is always a concern: don't take too much, or there won't be room in the car, or the bag will incur an airline surcharge, or you won't have room for presents. Make sure to pack toothbrush and toothpaste, change of clothes, phone charger...so we make lists. Backpackers, who must carry whatever they need, tend to be more efficient than those who go by car, plane, bus, or train. For the disciples, minimal essentials, and that's it.

Mark limits them to *one staff; no bread, no bag, and no in the belt bronze* [i.e., money]...*sandals, and [one] tunic[s]* (6:8-9). This isn't much. Matthew 10:9-10 affords them even less: not only no bag and only one tunic, but no sandals or staff. For Mark, the disciples are not without protection: a staff to ward away bandits or to help with climbing the Galileans hills; sandals to keep from blisters. But they are vulnerable. Without money, they must rely on others or live, like the Baptizer, off the land.

We can regard them as missional day laborers: they provide exorcism and the proclamation of the good news, and in turn they receive hospitality. Yet unlike day laborers, their lack of resources is voluntary rather than structural. They have extra tunics; they have bread and bags and bronze (Matthew 10:9 presumes that they have "gold, silver, and copper" to bring, and then mandates that they take no money on the road). They leave these behind; the disciples voluntarily make themselves vulnerable and dependent.

Personally, I would not invite two strangers into my home to discuss the gospel, or to provide exorcisms. I have, however, sat with missionaries on my porch (after I check their IDs and give a brief theological quiz to check their legitimacy). I give them pointers in evangelizing; if they are going to do it, they should do it well. For Mark's missionary model to work, there must be trust on the part of both disciple and householder.

> **For Mark's missionary model to work, there must be trust on the part of both disciple and householder.**

I've read a few sermons proclaiming that the packing model is from Exodus, since concerning the escape from Egypt, Exodus 12:11 instructs the Israelites to eat the Passover lamb with "your sandals on your feet, and your staff in your hand." This connection strikes me as derived from a creative use of a concordance, to see where else "staff" and "sandals" show up; I do not see the mission as a new Exodus. The disciples are, for a time, leaving the company of Jesus, not leaving slavery. They are not passing through the Red Sea; they are passing through Galilean villages. Moreover, later sources suggest that Jews were reclining to eat the Passover meal, since reclining at table is what non-enslaved people do. Hence, Mark 14:18 (NIV) describes Jesus and his disciples as "reclining" at the Last Supper, which for Mark is a Passover seder.

Whatever provision the disciples receive requires engagement with others. It also requires a personal touch that today's systems of charity do not have. There's a difference between inviting a homeless and hungry person into our homes and donating to Habitat for Humanity or Room in the Inn. Again, Jesus does not make discipleship easy. Perhaps people in small villages in Galilee were more trusting, and more hospitable, than people in big cities in the United States.

Jesus anticipates that the disciples will receive home hospitality: *Wherever you might enter into a house, there remain until when you might go out from there* (6:10). In other words, do not search for better accommodations. Such a move both embarrasses the original host and suggests that the disciples are more invested in social prestige and better food than in exorcisms and healing.

Food will need to be shared. Space for sleeping will need to be provided. Jesus anticipates that both food and space will be available: to send two able-bodied (as far as we know) disciples into areas with food insecurity and thus insist that two more mouths be fed, perhaps at the expense of the children who might go hungry, would be, in my view, sinful. Lower Galilee in the late 20s experienced no famine or drought. There was enough to go around.

We can also appreciate the risk the householder takes in inviting the disciples, not in terms of crime but in terms of reputation. For the householder, hosting the disciples could bring social stigma. Jesus's own family wanted to take him away from public performances (Mark 3:21). More, exorcists deal with demons, and who needs that? Jesus has already separated husbands from wives and sons from parents—Peter from his wife or at least his mother-in-law (Mark 1:30-31); James and John from their father (Mark 1:19-20)—so his presence or the presence of his followers has potential to disrupt the household. I can imagine young adults telling their parents with whom they worked, "I'm going with Peter and Andrew to go fish for people." I can imagine the parents having some choice words for Peter and Andrew.

Conversely, the householder who receives a disciple may receive honor from others in the village: it was at *your* house where the exorcism took place; it was at *your* house where the good news was proclaimed, and sinners repented. Risk and reward are not mutually exclusive.

Jesus continues his instruction, now concerning situations where the disciples are not welcomed: *whichever a place not having received you, neither having listened to you, when you are going out from there, shake off the dust beneath your feet in witness to them* (6:11). I like this idea. Many years ago, when I was dealing with a very difficult fellow faculty member, I would write his initials on the soles of my running shoes and then hit the track. By the end of my run, those initials were wiped off, and I felt better. Sometimes there's nothing you can do, when your words are not welcome, other than to say "bye-bye" and move on. Jesus wants people to repent, but if folks are not going to listen to the message, there's no reason for missionaries either to harass or to beat their heads against the wall.

On occasion, commentators will assert that the Jews who returned to Israel after traveling in the Diaspora would shake the dust off their feet and so remove any sources of "uncleanness." I could find no direct evidence of such a practice. I did find, from the Zohar, a medieval text of Jewish mysticism, the notice that at the general resurrection of the dead, God will shake the dust off the revivified bodies (good to know).

Everything apparently worked out well for our intrepid Twelve. *They proclaimed that they might repent. And many demons they were casting out, and they were anointing with oil many sick people, and they were healing* (6:12-13). No signs of rejection; no failed exorcisms. All good. They even supplement Jesus's teaching, since the anointing with oil is not something he had either recommended or practiced. However, a similar concern surfaces in the Epistle of James (which really should be called the Epistle of Jacob), a text that has many connections with Gospel accounts of Jesus. James 5:14 teaches that anyone in the church who is sick should summon the elders, who would pray over them and *anoint [them] with oil in the name of the Lord.*

We might think of this anointing as a prayer tool, a tactile feeling of connection, something that would make the ailing person not only feel good but feel welcomed by fellow congregants. To be anointed with oil is literally to be in good hands, and in various ways, whether for health care or hospitality or honor. Psalm 23:5, the famous "The LORD is my shepherd" psalm, exclaims, *You grease with oil my head* (the King James Version, "*thou anointest my head with oil,"* sounds better*)*. Placing oil on the hair was a sign of luxury, as depicted for example in Ecclesiastes 9:8, *And oil upon your head do not lack.* When an anonymous woman puts nard, a type of oil, on Jesus's head in Mark 14:3, she could have intended to honor him; he interprets the oil as an anticipation of his burial.

> **To be anointed with oil is literally to be in good hands, and in various ways, whether for health care or hospitality or honor.**

At the conclusion of this missionary endeavor, Mark states, *came together the apostles to Jesus.* This is the first and only time Mark refers to them as *apostles,* from the Greek *apostellō,* to "send out." Here they fulfilled their apostolic commission. *They announced to [Jesus] all that they had done and what they had taught* (6:30). Their success bodes well for the future of the movement. It also hints that despite the failure of all Twelve at the end of the Gospel narrative, eleven of them will regroup.

But in between the mission and this announcement of success comes the Baptizer's beheading.

Herod Antipas, Herodias, the Dancing Daughter, and John the Baptizer (Mark 6:14-29)

In the Gospel's only scene in which Jesus is not the main character, we meet the ruler of Galilee, Herod Antipas, his wife and niece Herodias, and her daughter. Unnamed in Mark's Gospel, she is in later tradition identified by the name Salome. Oscar Wilde, and then Richard Strauss, connect her with the dance of the seven veils. While the sexy striptease worked for the very self-aware Rita Hayworth in the 1953 film *Salome,* the scene in Mark 6 is, for various reasons, more disturbing than it is entertaining.

The narrative begins as Herod Antipas, called "king" by Mark but in fact a "tetrarch," a ruler of one-fourth of a kingdom, hears about the healings and exorcisms performed by Jesus and his followers. The story is told as a flashback:

> *And heard the King Herod, for known had become his [Jesus's] name, and they were saying that John the Baptizer had been raised from the dead, and on account of this, are working these powers in him.*

> *But others were saying Elijah he is, and others were saying that a prophet, as one of the prophets.*

> *But hearing, Herod said, [this one] whom I beheaded, John, this one has been raised. For Herod himself having sent, seized John, bound him in prison on account of Herodias, the wife of Philip his brother, because her he married. For he had been saying, John, to Herod, that "it is not permitted to you to have the wife of your brother."*

> *And Herodias had a grudge against him and wanted him to kill. But she was not able. For Herod was fearing John, knowing him a man righteous and holy, and he preserved him. And when he heard him, he was much at a loss, and [yet] with pleasure he heard him.*

> *And came an opportune day, when Herod, on his birthday, a drinking party he made for his magisterial ones and commanders and for the first of Galilee. And when she came in, his daughter, of Herodias, and dancing, she pleased Herod and those who reclined with him, and said the king to the girl, "Ask me for whatever you wish, and I will give to you." And he took an oath [a lot] to her, "Whatever you ask me, I will give to you, even half of my kingdom."*

> *And going out, she said to her mother, "What should I ask?" And she said, "The head of John the Baptizer."*

> *And she, going in, immediately, with haste, to the king asked, saying that "I want you, quickly, to give me on a platter the head of John the Baptizer."*

> *And sorry becoming, the king, on account of his oaths and the co-recliners, did not wish to reject her. And immediately, sending, the*

king, an executioner, ordered to bring his head, and going out, he beheaded him in the prison. And he brought his head upon a platter, and he gave it to the girl, and the girl gave it to her mother.

And hearing, his disciples, they came, and they took his corpse and they put it in a tomb.

Given that the previous narrative in Mark concerns the mission of the Twelve, it is possible that their activities brought *[Jesus's] name* to Antipas's attention. Jesus had avoided Tiberias, the city Antipas built, in part, to rival the building enterprises of his father, Herod the Great. By calling Antipas *Herod*, Mark may be contrasting the politically savvy father with the less astute son. I'll call the tetrarch Antipas so we do not confuse him with his father.

Jesus had also issued commands to keep the miracles secret. Mark's message is clear: proclaim a Messiah and do deeds of mighty power in his name, and authorities will notice, not in a good way.

Just as the Twelve wonder about Jesus's identity, so does Antipas. In modern idiom, he asks, "Who is this guy?" His advisors are ready with answers, none correct. Some suggest that Jesus is Elijah, the prophet whose appearance would inaugurate the messianic age. But, as we readers know, Mark assigns that role to John. Others propose that Jesus is a prophet, or even the reincarnation of one of the ancient prophets, such as Isaiah or Jeremiah. The idea of reincarnation, or transmigration of souls, was one option in first-century Jewish thought.

Still others propose that Jesus is John raised from the dead. This cue then segues into Mark's story of how John died. Questions about Jesus's identity will continue in the rest of the Gospel. In Mark 8:27-28, Jesus asks his disciples what they have heard people saying about him. The disciples respond that some think he is John the Baptizer; others Elijah, and still others one of the prophets. When Jesus asks who the disciples think he is, Peter—unexpectedly, given his obtuseness elsewhere—answers, *You are the Christ* [i.e., Messiah]

(Mark 8:29). This is the first use of that title since the superscription. Incorrect answers about Jesus's identity lead to Antipas's banquet; the correct answer, he is the Christ, leads to the Last Supper.

In terms of the details of John's death, whether Mark's account is "what happened" or whether Mark has combined the fact of John's death with anti-Herodian propaganda, will remain debated. I find historically credible the account of John's death Josephus records in his *Antiquities of the Jews* 18.116-119. Josephus states that Antipas became alarmed by John's popularity and executed him as a preemptive strike lest he lead the people into rebellion.

But Josephus does include a notice connecting John's death to Antipas's marriage. When he married Herodias, Antipas set aside his (unnamed) current wife, the daughter of Aretas IV, king of Nabatea, a small region bordering the Galilee. Aretas, furious with this treatment of his daughter, declared war against Antipas. Josephus reports that Antipas's defeat in the ensuing battle was punishment for his execution of John.

Mark's version involves not John's popularity but his preaching: Antipas arrested John *on account of Herodias, the wife of Philip his brother, because her he married. For he had been saying, John, to Herod, that "it is not permitted to you to have the wife of your brother"* (6:18-19). Leviticus 18:16 mandates, *The nakedness of the wife of your brother you shall not uncover* or, colloquially, "Don't have sexual relations with your brother's wife." John thus accuses Antipas of incest.

Whereas Josephus suggests that Antipas harbors fear of and enmity toward John, Mark depicts the tetrarch as ambivalent. The hatred, according to Mark, belongs to Herodias: *And Herodias had a grudge against him, and wanted him to kill. But she was not able. For Herod was fearing John, knowing him a man righteous and holy, and he preserved him. And when he heard him, he was much at a loss, and [yet] with pleasure he heard him* (6:19-20).

The story looks like a reprise of 2 Kings 16-21, the story of Queen Jezebel, the enemy of Elijah. Just as Jezebel manipulated her husband, King Ahab, so Herodias manipulates Antipas. Just as Elijah indicts Ahab and Jezebel, so John the Baptizer indicts Antipas and Herodias.

Herodias wants the Baptizer silenced, but Antipas protects him. Then Antipas hosts a party to celebrate his birthday. The opening line, concerning the *drinking party he made for his magisterial ones and commanders and for the first of Galilee*, echoes the opening of the Book of Esther, where the (also-manipulated-by-his-wives [pl.]) King Ahasuerus of Persia holds a drinking party for "*all his princes and his servants, the army of Persia and Media, the nobles and the princes of the provinces*" (Esther 1:3).

In the story of Esther, Ahasuerus is furious with Queen Vashti's refusal to appear before him and his equally intoxicated guests (one legend suggests that he wanted her to appear wearing her royal crown, but only her royal crown). On the advice of his courtiers, he deposes Vashti, holds an all-Persia beauty contest, and makes the beautiful Esther, a Jew who, instructed by her guardian Mordecai, keeps her ethnicity secret (as Jesus tried to keep his messianic identity secret). Ahasuerus, smitten with Esther, promises her that whatever she asks, *until half of the kingdom, and it will be given to you* (Esther 5:3); he repeats the promise in 5:6 and 7:2. Similarly, Antipas, impressed with the daughter's dancing, swears to her, *Whatever you ask me, I will give to you, even half of my kingdom* (Mark 6:23). The connections to Esther, already secure, are reinforced by the motif of irrevocable commandments. In the Book of Esther, Haman, the villain, manipulates the king into signing a death warrant for Persia's Jews. When Esther finally informs the king that he has condemned her people to death, he explains that Persian laws cannot be revoked. Antipas, who did not want John killed, is unable to revoke his promise to the daughter: to revoke a public oath would risk shame and diminish his authority. Mark is running the plot of the Book of Esther.

The daughter is, in Greek, a *korasion*, the same term Mark uses for Jairus's twelve-year-old daughter whom Jesus raised from the dead in the previous chapter. The Greek translation of the Book of Esther not only identifies Esther as a *korasion* (Esther 2:7, 9 and elsewhere), it uses this term for the "virgins" that the king gathers to the palace to find a new bride (2:2 and elsewhere). Thus, we can see Esther and Herodias's daughter as twelve-year-olds! This scene seems prurient to me, and it likely would have felt the same for Mark's readers. Not only is the dancer a child, but she is also Antipas's stepdaughter. Nor should a princess royal be entertaining Antipas and his blitzed officers: the scene is a drinking party, not a family dinner where doting parents invite their children to play "Twinkle, Twinkle Little Star" on the violin (I am guilty here).

Herod Antipas and Herodias are well matched. He, inappropriately, lusts for the girl; she, inappropriately, uses the girl to achieve her own ends: The daughter *said to her mother, "What should I ask?" And she said, "The head of John the baptizer"* (Mark 6:24). The notice evokes other beheadings and related scenes, especially scenes prompted by women. According to the Song of Deborah, Jael *her hand to the tent peg she sent, and her right hand to the workers' hammer; and she struck Sisera, she destroyed his head, and she shattered and pierced his temple* (Judges 5:26). Judith first beguiles the enemy general Holofernes and then, when he is drunk, beheads him with his own sword (Judith 13:8). She even packs the head in a food-bag and brings it home with her (Judith 13:10). On the pagan side, several Roman historians record an incident where an official, seeking to please a courtesan at a banquet, complied with her wish to see a person beheaded. The historians found the whole episode disgusting. Right.

Herodias's daughter returns immediately and announces to Antipas, *I want you, quickly, to give me on a platter the head of John the Baptizer* (Mark 6:25). The platter was her own idea. She does not question her mother's desire for John's death; she adds to it. She thus transforms John into another course at the banquet, more food imagery, but of a most perverse menu. She should have asked for a pony.

Because Antipas admires John, to kill him is to act against his own interests. He allows himself to be manipulated by wife and daughter. While history tends to blame Herodias—blaming the "evil woman" is an easy and common move—the person finally responsible for John's death is the tetrarch or, in Mark's account, the *king*. His *oaths, and the co-recliners*, that is, his guests, are more important than justice. So, too, the person responsible for the death of Jesus is, ultimately, Pontius Pilate, and not the people who, according to Mark's narrative, manipulated him. John's beheading thus anticipates Jesus's crucifixion. Here the Nicene Creed, a text that unites a variety of Christian groups, correctly includes the line, "For our sake he was crucified under Pontius Pilate."

With Antipas's banquet, Mark also sets up contrasts to other Gospel meals. For example, we have seen how the word *korasion* describes the daughters of Jairus and Herodias. The two scenes are also distinct in that they are the only scenes in Mark depicting a father, mother, and daughter. But while Jesus raises Jairus's daughter and then orders that she be given something to eat (Mark 5:43), Herodias's daughter sets up a murder and then brings her mother an inedible dish.

Antipas's banquet is also a perverse Eucharist: John's head is served to satisfy Herodias's deadly resentment; Jesus at the Last Supper inaugurates a meal that brings his followers life and unity.

To get the taste of Antipas's banquet out of our mouths, Mark serves, as the next story, the feeding of the five thousand (Mark 6:31-44). In place of Antipas and his A-list officials are Galilean Jews gathered as Mark 6:34 puts it, *as sheep not having a shepherd*. Instead of a lavish banquet there is only bread and fish, but instead of the cannibalistic and the inedible, the food Jesus provides, like manna in the wilderness, satisfies all.

The grisly story of Antipas's banquet ends with the notice that John's disciples *took his corpse and they put it in a tomb* (6:29). Mark sets up an ironic, and tragic contrast to the death of Jesus, who is buried by Joseph of Arimathea, a stranger. John's disciples remain faithful; Jesus's disciples betray him, deny him, and desert him. John's death anticipates the cross: a popular teacher who accuses people in authority of illegal behavior is arrested and then killed. There is behind-the-scenes manipulation, authorities who act from cowardice or from fear, soldiers who murder an innocent man because, well, they were just following orders. Death at the hands of corrupt authorities is the fate of John, and Jesus, and of countless others who have done the right thing, at the cost of their own lives.

> **Death at the hands of corrupt authorities is the fate of John, and Jesus, and of countless others who have done the right thing, at the cost of their own lives.**

What Creates Uncleanness (Mark 7:1-23)

Our final text for this chapter introduces more concerns for eating: here the issue is less the what, the where, or even the who, but the how. Jesus debates Pharisees over their practice of handwashing (after Covid, who knew—the Pharisees had the right idea!), and that discussion segues into an argument that uses the language of ritual purity to speak of what we might call moral purity. To understand this long (twenty-three verses) account requires knowledge of who the Pharisees were, why they developed new laws, and why Jesus resisted their changes. At the end of the story, I find myself agreeing with both the Pharisees (on handwashing) and with Jesus (on speaking). I also find lessons about the importance of ritual, the need to reformulate traditions under new circumstances, the value of debate, and the importance of knowing how texts might have taken shape in historical context.

We start with our text, Mark 7:1-23:

And having come together to him Pharisees and some of the scribes coming from Jerusalem, and seeing some of his disciples that with common hands, that is, not washed, they were eating bread. For the Pharisees, and all the Jews, unless by a fist they might wash the hands, do not eat, observing the tradition of the elders; and from the market unless they wash not do they eat; and there are also many other traditions to observe, the washing of cups, pots, and bronze kettles.

And they ask him, the Pharisees and the scribes, "On account of why not do they walk around your disciples according to the tradition of the elders, but with common hands do they eat?"

He said to them, "Rightly prophesied Isaiah about you hypocrites, as it is written [that], 'This people with their lips honors me, but their hearts are far away from me; in vain they worship me, teaching as teachings commandments of human beings.' Abandoning the commandment of God, you grasp the tradition of human beings."

And he was saying to them, "Well do you reject the commandment of God in order your tradition you might keep! For Moses said, 'Honor your father and your mother' and, 'the one speaking evil of father or mother by death let him die.' But you say, 'If might say a person to father or to mother, qorban, which is a gift, that from me you might benefit.' No longer do you permit it nothing to do for the father or the mother. Cancelling the word of God by your tradition [what was handed over (paradosis) which you have handed over (paradidomi)]. And many things like this you do."

And calling together again the crowd, he was saying to them, "Listen to me, all of you, and understand: nothing is outside a human being going in him which is able to make common [defile] him, but the things that out of a human being are coming are what makes common [defile] the human being."

["If anyone has ears to hear, let him hear."]

When he had gone into a house from the crowd, were asking him his disciples the parable. And he says to them, "Thus even you are without understanding? [!] Not do you know that all that is from outside going into a human being not is able him to make common, because not does it enter him into the heart but into the belly, and into the latrine it goes out?" [thus] making clean all foods.

> *And he was saying that, "What out of a human being comes, that makes common [defiles] the human being. For it is within, out of the heart of human beings, that evil intentions come: sexual (sin), theft, murder, adultery, greed, wickedness, deceit, indecency, evil eye, blasphemy, pride, foolishness. All these evil things from within coming out, and they make common [defile] a human being."*

We begin with the Pharisees, Mark's stock villains until we reach the Passion Narrative, when the chief priests and elders take over the antagonists' role. I picture Mark's Gospel being read in the home of a Gentile Christian patron; each time the narrator mentions Pharisees, the crowd boos. Yet the Pharisees were popular teachers at the time of Jesus and some, notably Paul of Tarsus, joined the movement. Paul does not cease to be a Pharisee after his Road-to-Damascus encounter with the Christ; rather, he becomes a Pharisee convinced that the messianic age has begun. When Mark's story is placed in historical context, we can better see what is going on in this discussion. We can also see why Matthew, likely better informed about Jewish practice than Mark, changed Mark's wording.

Mark describes how *Pharisees and some of the scribes* (7:1), likely having heard about Jesus, were coming *from Jerusalem*. The geographical notice portends danger in the city. We are not yet in the Passion Narrative, but the seeds are planted.

The Pharisees are concerned with the disciples' disregard of a popular practice. They were *seeing some of his disciples that with common hands, that is, not washed, they were eating bread* (7:2). Simply put: Jesus's disciples did not wash their hands before they ate. The charge is not leveled against Jesus. In Mark 2:23-24, the Pharisees questioned why the disciples, but not Jesus, were winnowing grain and thus behaving in a way counter to how they understood celebrating the Sabbath. It is possible that such disagreements about how to engage practices related to eating and to Sabbath-keeping reflect not Jesus's own practice but the practices of his (Gentile) followers.

Mark then offers an inaccurate or at least exaggerated explanation: *For the Pharisees, and all the Jews, unless by a fist they might wash the hands, do not eat, observing the tradition of the elders; and from the market unless they wash not do they eat; and but there are also many other traditions to observe, the washing of cups, pots, and bronze kettles* (7:3-4). Extrapolating from Pharisaic practice to "all Jews" is the first problem, since Jesus and the disciples are clearly Jews, and the disciples are not washing.

The second problem is that the practice is often misunderstood. A number of my students think that all first-century Jews, save Jesus, suffered from obsessive-compulsive disorder such that they were continually washing their hands. That is the wrong impression. The Pharisees are concerned with sanctity, not neurosis. Just as the priests in the Jerusalem Temple washed their hands before approaching the altar, so the Pharisees promoted an egalitarianism in which everyone could act like a priest (see Exodus 30) even if they were not in the Temple or from a priestly family. Since Exodus 19:6 speaks of Israel as a "kingdom of priests, and an holy nation" (KJV), the idea of extending priestly privileges to the people made sense.

By the way, the priestly practice of washing one's hands prior to coming into contact with elements of the holy continues in those churches today in which people presiding over the Eucharist (or Communion) symbolically wash their hands. The point is not hygiene; if it were, they'd be using soap, or alcohol-based cleanser. The point is ritual purity.

Practices such as handwashing, along with circumcision, dietary observances, Sabbath observances, using chalkstone rather than ceramic vessels, avoiding anthropomorphic depictions, etc., were the means by which Jews preserved their identity, despite exile or Diaspora existence, despite being ruled by a succession of non-Jewish governments: Babylon, Persia, Greece, pagan Rome, Christian Rome, and so on. By no means burdensome, these practices enabled Jews to affirm their identity, resist assimilation, and sanctify their bodies.

> **Practices such as handwashing, along with circumcision, dietary observances, Sabbath observances, using chalkstone rather than ceramic vessels, avoiding anthropomorphic depictions, etc., were the means by which Jews preserved their identity.**

Pharisees were also interested in making practice easier to follow, so much so that the Dead Sea Scrolls refer to them as "seekers after smooth things." For the authors of the Scrolls, Pharisees make things too easy. Here is why the reference to the *fist* makes sense. Pouring water over a fist is more efficient than attempting to cover the back of an open hand (feel free to try this if you wish). The issue is symbolism, not hygiene. The Pharisees thus pose a legitimate question concerning the disciples: *why... with common hands do they eat?* (7:5) Why don't the disciples wash? Do they not see themselves as members of a holy nation? Are they not interested in extending priestly privilege? While not a perfect analogy, we might compare this move to the practice, in some Christian communions, of allowing or even encouraging anyone, and not just ordained clergy, to distribute the Eucharist (Communion). Some people in the congregation might find this freeing; others might find it horrifying.

When it comes to fidelity to Torah, everyone adapted, since all laws require interpretation. We in the United States can be "faithful" to our Constitution, but we also have amendments that also require attention. Pharisees had what Mark calls the *traditions of the elders* (7:5); Sadducees, John the Baptizer and his disciples, Essenes, and other Jewish groups had their own traditions. Jesus, like the Pharisees, adapts the tradition and sometimes adds to it. For example, in the Sermon on the Mount, he adds to the law against murder an injunction against anger; to the law against adultery, he adds an injunction against lust (Matthew 5:21-30). In Mark, he adds a prohibition against divorce and remarriage. For later additions, we might consider the Roman Catholic magisterium, Calvin's *Institutes*, the Methodist *Book of Discipline*, and so on. Practices continue to change as new issues confront ecclesial communities.

Jesus now goes on the offensive both to protect his disciples and to contest Pharisaic practice. He calls the Pharisees hypocrites and then quotes Isaiah against them. The citation, *This people with their lips honor me, but their heart is far from me, in vain do they worship me, teaching as teachings* [i.e., a doctrine] *commandments of people*, is to the Greek translation of Isaiah 29:13. When Jews criticize other Jews, or when we read Isaiah in the synagogue, we recognize the critique as insider-language, as parents might critique a child. But when Isaiah's words, or Jesus's words, are taken out of their Jewish context and put into a text that becomes part of the (Gentile) Christian canon, the effect is not insider critique designed to help people get back on the right path; the effect can be external polemic. We all get off track at one time or another; we all need sharp words to wake us up.

Next, Jesus attempts to show how the tradition of the elders, how updating, can lead to abusive behavior. He begins by citing Torah: *Moses said, 'Honor your father and your mother' and 'the one speaking evil of father or mother by death let him die'* (7:10). One might quibble and say that Jesus's comments redefining the family (Mark 3:32-34 also 10:29) are not indicative of honoring. Rather than quibble, since the *tu quoque* argument (i.e., you do bad things too) is not often helpful, we turn to the specifics of his case.

To make his point, Jesus adduces the practice of *qorban*, or dedicating something to the Temple. The system could be misused. For example, if one vows something to the Temple—the proceeds of the next harvest, coins, jewelry, whatever—its monetary value cannot be used to support parents. A modern equivalent would be making a pledge to a worthy cause. While vowing something to the Temple (or to a church, for that matter) does not prevent supporting parents in other ways, Jesus has a point. People make extravagant gifts to charitable organizations with the impact of leaving less to, or even impoverishing, their own families. Consequently, the Mishnah, Nedarim 9.1, insists that any vow that would create difficulties for one's parents can be annulled. Jesus wasn't the only one paying attention to how pledges can become destructive.

Jesus now changes the subject: *Nothing is outside a human being going in him which is able to make common [defile] him, but the things that out of a human being are coming is what makes common [defile] a human being* (7:14). While I regret the awkwardness of the translation as well as the androcentric "him" since no one, on the basis of gender, is free from such defiling, I agree with Jesus's point. Technically, he is correct, since dietary regulations do not function on the same register as do other purity laws. Purity laws in general concern impermanent everyday states regarding life and death, such as menstruation, ejaculation, and childbirth. Purity is regained after ritual immersion. Just as there are circumstances that create impurity, so there are means of regaining purity, such as waiting until sundown and going to the ritual bath (*miqveh*). That is not the case with diet. On the one hand, we have greater control over what we eat than over what our body does naturally. On the other, there is no ritual action that restores purity after eating something that is not kosher.

That *were asking him his disciples* about *the parable* shows that the disciples realized that Jesus is neither making a law nor abrogating one. He is not saying, "Therefore, go order a ham and cheese with mayonnaise"; he is speaking metaphorically, in *a parable*, about how what we say can be defiling.

Jesus is frustrated with the disciples (I would be too): *Thus even you are not understanding.* I'm not sure whether this is a question ("Are you still clueless?") or an exclamation ("Even you are clueless!"). He explains, *all that is from outside going into a human being not is able him to make common, because not does it enter him into the heart but into the womb/stomach, and into the latrine it goes out?"* (7:18-19).

What one eats does not make one unclean: what goes in eventually comes out; it does not create a permanent state.

This statement does not mean that Jesus was *making clean all foods* or as some translations read, "declaring all foods clean" in the sense of doing away with dietary regulations. Were he to do so, he would be guilty of *abandoning the commandment of God*, precisely the charge he levels against the Pharisees. (It seems weird to me, but my students almost never notice this point. Jesus does not abandon any of the commandments; he rather makes them stricter.) Mark has mistaken an analogy, a parable, for a pronouncement. Had Jesus abrogated the dietary laws, he would also be defaming the memory of the Jewish martyrs, put to death for refusing to *eat what is common* [i.e., unclean food] and *desecrate the holy covenant* (1 Maccabees 1:62-63). Had Jesus eliminated kashrut, then the Apostolic Council of Acts 15, in which his followers discuss whether *gentiles* need to follow Jewish dietary laws, is unintelligible. Had he done away with dietary laws, then his statement in Matthew 5:17, where he makes clear that he did not *come to abolish the Law and the Prophets*" makes no sense. And if he did abolish kashrut, then it is odd that no one in Mark makes any comment about it. In rewriting this passage, Matthew correctly omits Mark's phrasing about declaring all foods clean (see Matthew 15:20).

Paul recognizes in his majority-Gentile congregations that some people maintain certain dietary regulations. In Romans 14:20 he acknowledges with Jesus that *everything on the one hand is clean*. The point follows from the idea that all of creation is good, since that it was God who pronounces in Genesis 1; that is the message from the famous Psalm 24:1a, *To the Lord* [YHWH/kyrios] *is the earth, and the fullness of it* [the King James Version has the famous, "The earth *is* the Lord's, and the fulness thereof"]. But while everything is intrinsically clean, Jews still follow the dietary laws. The practice is not for hygiene, although sometimes it worked out that way, but for cultural or ethnic identity.

For a not-quite-full analogy, but one that my students find helpful, we can look how different cultures understand diet. In France, horsemeat is sold in supermarkets; not in the United States. There is nothing "unclean" about eating puppies and kittens, but most of us would gag at the idea (as I am typing, my dog is lying next to me; she isn't thrilled with the idea either). What is "permitted" is not necessarily what is "desirable."

Jesus then speaks of impurity as a moral concern: *"What out of a human being comes, that makes common [defiles] the human being. For it is within, out of the heart of human beings, that evil intentions come out"* (7:21). Using the language of ritual purity to make a statement about morality, Jesus is speaking parabolically. He adapts the tradition, just as John the Baptizer adapted the ritual of immersion for ritual purity into a ritual designating repentance. Jesus did not do away with dietary laws any more than John did away with the practice of ritual immersion.

The sense of feeling "dirty" in the presence of immoral action, one takeaway from Jesus's statement, makes sense to me. Several years ago, before marriage equality became the law in the United States, I was asked to testify in family court on what the Bible says about same-sex sexual relations. The case concerned a divorced father who wanted to share with his ex-wife custody of their children. The ex-wife, a fundamentalist Christian, wanted to revoke his custody because he had come out as gay. Watching two people fight over their children made me feel dirty (I took a shower as soon as I got home from court). Jesus's comment regarding what creates moral impurity—evil intentions leading to actions that harm others— seems like a good definition to me.

Mark 7 finally tells us that we should attend both to what we eat and with whom we eat. The message is as relevant today as it was two millennia ago. Do we invite people who have violated community welfare (we might remember those tax collectors and sinners) to our tables, or do we keep them away? Do we socialize with people who have violated community welfare because they have the best parties, or because we want to be photographed with them, or do we take the invitation as an opportunity to encourage repentance? (If so, we'll be off the A-list quickly.) Are we eating food that *should* be listed as inedible, such as from an endangered species? And as we are at table—at the altar; in the fellowship hall; at the picnic—do we attend to what we say? Does our table welcome and reconcile, or have we recreated Antipas's banquet, which is spectacle, prurience, and death?

CHAPTER 3

Sacrifice, Ransom, Prophet, Messiah

Mark 8–10

Mark 8, halfway through the Gospel's sixteen chapters, represents a turning point. From speaking in parables and commanding people to remain silent about his mighty works, Jesus now speaks *plainly*, and his message is not one of miracle but of martyrdom. In Mark 8, Jesus predicts his suffering, death, and then resurrection, and the Gospel begins to move inexorably to the cross. Again, insiders prove obtuse, and outsiders understand him. We readers again will understand more than the disciples do, but even we may be unprepared for some of Jesus's actions and statements.

Mark 8 begins with the feeding of the four thousand; the setting suggests predominantly Gentile territory. It appears that the man whom Jesus exorcised of that Legion of demons has laid the groundwork for this second trip across the Sea of Galilee. That this second miraculous feeding follows Jesus's exorcism, at a distance, of the daughter of a Greek woman (Syro-Phoenician by birth) indicates the role Gentiles will play in what comes to be called the "church" (in Greek, *ekklesia*, whence "ecclesiastical"; Mark does not use the term). Mark's Jesus mandates no Gentile mission; Matthew 28:16-20, the "Great Commission," is based on Jesus's own change in status now that he has *all authority* (Matthew 28:18) following his resurrection; Luke reserves the Gentile mission for the Book of Acts; John has no missionary mandate. Jesus is not, at the beginning of Mark 8, "transgressing" ethnic boundaries (a common preaching trope since it sounds inclusive; it also functions illegitimately to differentiate Jesus from his fellow Jews, seen as xenophobic). He did not begin a mission to the Gentiles, although he signaled in his healings, exorcisms, and teachings, that the Gentiles are also part of God's creation. Like his fellow Jews, he probably envisioned the Gentiles as turning to the God of Israel by divine fiat at the eschaton.

Following the two-stage healing of the blind man in Bethsaida, we come to Peter's confession of Jesus's messianic identity and Jesus's first Passion prediction, which continues into Mark 9. Because the third Passion prediction comes in Mark 10, we'll hold discussion of this material for the end of our chapter.

Mark 9 goes from the pathos of the Passion predictions to the triumph of the Transfiguration or, for Mark, the magnificence of the Metamorphosis (9:2-13), our first text for discussion, together with Jesus's announcement that some of his disciples will not taste death before they see the Kingdom come in power. Next comes the healing of a demon-possessed boy, a scene that complicates, in what I think is a helpful way, the role of faith, the abilities of the disciples, and the emotions Jesus displays (9:14-29). Therefore, we'll take some time to unpack this remarkable text. The rest of Mark 9 features a second Passion prediction, the disciples' misguided question about who among them was the greatest, and the general teachings about how to proclaim the Gospel.

Finally, in Mark 10, Jesus continues his teaching: forbidding divorce, blessing the children and instructing his followers to become like little children, the rich man who seeks to inherit eternal life, and then the third Passion prediction (10:32-34). Despite Jesus's focus on his death, and despite his announcement that he will die as a ransom for many (10:45), the disciples are more interested in jockeying for position. Jesus instructs them in what might be called servant-leadership. The chapter ends with the healing of

Bar-Timaeus, a blind man in Jericho. For Mark 10, we look at the Passion predictions: Why does Jesus have to suffer? Why does Jesus have to die? To whom is the ransom paid? These are the questions I wish the disciples in Mark had asked. These are questions we may continue to ask. "Because it is God's will" is, for many of my students and, especially, for the youth with whom I work, an insufficient answer.

The Kingdom Come in Power (Mark 9:1)

We remain in the area of Caesarea-Philippi, where in Mark 8, Peter—in a striking moment of lucidity—confesses that Jesus is the Messiah. The confession prompts Jesus's first Passion prediction. Peter has the right title, but he has the wrong job description. In his view, the messianic task is to heal the sick, exorcise demons, and control the weather. To the contrary, Jesus tells him that he [Jesus] must suffer and die. Peter, finding the idea of a messiah not only dying but also suffering incomprehensible, attempts to deflect the claim. Jesus calls Peter "Satan" (not a compliment) and goes on to describe his role, and that of his followers: to serve rather than to be served.

The Metamorphosis, following the Passion prediction, provides assurance both of Jesus's divine identity and of the legitimacy of his statements. It also reinforces Jesus's connections to Moses and therefore to the Torah (had Jesus done away with the dietary regulations, he and Moses would have had a great deal more to talk about) and to Elijah and therefore to the Prophets.

Who Will Not Taste Death

How can we recognize the messianic age? The dead have not risen, there has been no final judgment, let alone an end to war, disease, or despair. Jesus states, immediately before he changes in appearance, *"Amen I say to you that [there] are some here standing who not will taste death until they see the Kingdom of God has come in power"* (Mark 9:1).

Unless we conclude that a few of the disciples never died (I find this conclusion unhelpful), then the coming of the Kingdom must have been seen by Jesus's disciples.

For some readers, the Kingdom comes with the growth of the church, that single seed with its enormous yield. Yet the disciples did not live to see the church take over the Roman Empire. More, church growth was not always benevolent. When slave owners converted, those they enslaved were expected to do the same. Not all conversion was voluntary. If the Kingdom coming in power means *forcing* people to worship in a certain way, that is not the type of Kingdom I want to celebrate.

When I was in graduate school, I heard the thesis that Mark's Metamorphosis was a retrojected Resurrection appearance. The Gospel ends with frightened women fleeing from an empty tomb but, so this argument goes, Mark did not want to leave readers without a glimpse of the resurrected body. Thus, Mark includes the Metamorphosis to assure readers that Jesus not only lived, but lives.

I'm not convinced. I can easily imagine the disciples experiencing the presence of Jesus in a mystical, visionary way. Nor does the Metamorphosis do what other Resurrection appearances do: it shows no worship by the disciples; it presents no commission. Nor does Jesus display the marks of the cross to show that he had died. Nor again is the Metamorphosis mutually exclusive to the Resurrection. In 2 Peter 1:17-18, the writer, in the name of Peter the apostle, recollects the *Bat Qol*, that heavenly voice, speaking of Jesus as the Beloved Son: *and this voice we ourselves heard carried from heaven while with him were on the holy mountain* (1:18). This text insists that the Metamorphosis is not a retrojected Resurrection appearance. To the contrary, the disciples remembered that they had seen something uncanny, and extraordinary.

Nor again am I convinced that Mark is here reflecting a belief in the imminence of the Parousia, the "appearance" or "second coming" of Jesus. Mark's readers knew that Jesus had not returned. Matthew and Luke wrote later than Mark, and they both (Matthew 16:28; Luke 9:27) include the comment that some of the disciples would not die before they saw the Kingdom manifest. Neither Gospel is expecting the return of Jesus a week from Tuesday.

If Mark 9:1 is not about Mark's need to show some sign of Jesus's divine identity prior to the cross, and it is not about the spread of the church or about the Second Coming, perhaps it suggests the *power* that can be experienced by those who take up Jesus's message of the Kingdom: of repentance, of care, of support. The message is therefore one of hope. Since it follows Jesus's prediction that *it is necessary that the Son of Humanity... be killed and after three days rise"* (Mark 8:31; also 9:31; 10:33-34 NRSVue), we can conclude that the Kingdom is experienced in both the cross (Jesus's willingness to die as a ransom for many) and the Resurrection (God's fidelity to Jesus).

For Mark, the Kingdom had come, is coming, and will come, with power. It has already come, powerfully, in the healings and exorcisms. It comes when human beings clean up their moral impurity. We can see that the Kingdom has come, in power, when people act in compassion rather than in selfishness, in generosity rather than in greed. The Kingdom *has come* when people who claim to be disciples act the part. The Kingdom *has come* when people of good will wrestle with difficult texts. The Kingdom *has come* when we repent of our mistakes and work to do better next time.

> **We can see that the Kingdom has come, in power, when people act in compassion rather than in selfishness, in generosity rather than in greed.**

And sometimes, the Kingdom has come when we experience something unbelievable, incredible, ineffable. We may not be able to articulate how we feel, but the feeling is there, nonetheless. For some, this feeling is love, whether for a life-partner, or a child welcomed to the family. For some, it is the love experienced when one feels the palpable presence of the divine. A friend, now deceased, described the loving care of a hospice nurse as making manifest Jesus's comment about *not tast[ing] death until they see the Kingdom of God* (Mark 9:1) real.

For Peter, James, and John, witnessing what is traditionally called the Transfiguration (only Luke uses the term) and what Mark calls a Metamorphosis would also have been seeing the kingdom of God come in power. Mark 9:1, placed immediately before the Metamorphosis, serves to interpret what follows. Whereas the disciples have difficulty believing that Jesus will die and so they cannot take the next step to accept his prediction of his being raised from the dead, they can now experience, before his Passion, part of his true nature. They see him in his full power and glory. That vision, fleeting as it is, may be enough to sustain them, and all disciples subsequently, as they wait for the Parousia.

The Metamorphosis (Mark 9:2-10)

Our context is Jesus's comment that some of his followers will not die before they see the Kingdom come. Some already have, including those disciples who exorcised demons, proclaimed the good news, and found welcome in homes in lower Galilee. Others who experienced the Kingdom included Peter's mother-in-law, numerous demon-possessed individuals, and others suffering in body and mind. But more is yet to come. The disciples Peter, James, and John will experience this Kingdom when they experience Jesus in his divine form. They do not, cannot, understand their vision as it is happening. Whether Mark's audience can is another question.

And after six days, Jesus took along Peter and James and John, and led them into a high mountain apart, by themselves. And he was metamorphosed before them. And his garments became shiny white exceedingly such that a cloth refiner upon the earth would not be able thus to whiten.

And appeared to them Elijah with Moses, and they were talking with Jesus.

And answering, Peter says to Jesus, "Rabbi, good it is for us here to be, and we might make three tents, one for you, and one for Moses, and one for Elijah." For not did he know what to answer, for they were afraid.

Then there was a cloud overshadowing them, and there was a voice out of the cloud, "This one is my Son, the beloved; hear him!"

And suddenly, when they looked around, no one did they see but Jesus, alone with them.

And when they were coming down the mountain, he commanded them that no one what they had seen to tell, until when the Son of Humanity out of the dead had risen.

And the word they grasped for themselves, seeking together what it is from the dead to rise.

And after six days, Jesus took along Peter and James and John, and led them into a high mountain apart, by themselves (9:2). "After six days" means after Peter's identification of Jesus as Messiah and Jesus's statement that he, the *Son of Humanity*, will suffer, die, and rise again. The disciples have had a week to process the information. They remain befuddled.

The timing is also a recollection of other events "after six days," especially the notice in Exodus 24:16, *And tented the glory of the* LORD [YHWH/kyrios] *upon Mount Sinai, and covered it the cloud six days. And he called to Moses on the seventh day from the midst of the cloud*: six days, Moses, a cloud, and a heavenly voice—the building blocks for Mark 9 are in place.

Sometimes, change of location helps encourage new perspectives. Jesus takes the three privileged disciples, Peter and James and John (I worry about Peter's brother, Andrew, who should be part of the group), to a high mountain. The setting recalls Mount Sinai, where Moses received God's Torah and delivered it to the people; Mount Horeb (another name for Sinai), where Elijah experienced the presence of God neither in the storm nor in the earthquake but in the still small voice, the silence, afterward (see 1 Kings 19 KJV). Matthew has seven mountain scenes, including the famous "Sermon on the Mount" and the setting of the Great Commission.

We do not know what mountain Mark had in mind. Early church tradition says the Transfiguration occurred on Mount Tabor. Given that there was a Roman fort on the mountain at the time of Jesus, this strikes me as an unlikely, albeit symbolically superb, setting. Mount Meron in Upper Galilee is possible, as is Mount Hermon, near Caesarea Philippi.

Mark has two other mountain scenes, but if we blink, we'll miss them. The first is Mark 3:13, where Jesus appoints the Twelve and gives them their commission. The instruction is provided away from the crowds who continue to seek Jesus's healing touch. While mountains can give the sense of being closer to God, as if God is "up" or "in heaven," for Mark, they also provide a place of privacy and intimacy. Away from the crowd, Jesus can offer instruction without interruption. Away from the crowd, the disciples can pay better attention. Mark's mountain scenes suggest to me clergy retreats: change the scene, renew and refresh.

Mark's second reference is at 6:46, when Jesus says farewell to the crowds in Bethsaida and goes *to the mountain to pray.* Now Jesus too needs the renewal moment. The next scene is his walking on the water. The mountain, and the prayer, lead to an eruption of the uncanny, or the miraculous. Go up the mountain, and you may be a different person when you return. While the bear who went over the mountain only saw the other side of the mountain (does anyone remember this song?), we are not bears and we should be awake rather than hibernating. We can understand a change in perspective.

Finally, in Mark 11:23 Jesus tells his disciples, *"Whoever might say to this mountain, 'Be taken up and thrown into the sea' and not doubt in his heart but have faith/truth that what he says will be, it will be to him.*" I wrestle with this other mountain reference. First, other than needing to move a mountain for purposes of road construction, I don't see people walking around saying, "Mountain, be moved." Second, such a prayer would be testing God, which is not a good thing. Third, the announcement creates psychological problems, since perfect faith or trust, if there were such a thing, no more moves mountains than it stops armies from destruction or disease from devastation. Some commentators suggest that Jesus is encouraging his disciples to pray for the destruction of Mount Zion, where the Jerusalem Temple stood. Such a prayer strikes me as at best uncharitable. Perhaps it might be better to think of this saying as a metaphor or a parable: faith—in God, in the right thing, in morality, in justice—gives us the ability to do what may seem impossible.

The disciples, on the mountain, see something unearthly: *And he was metamorphosed before them. And his garments became shiny white exceedingly such that a cloth refiner upon the earth would not be able thus to whiten* (Mark 9:2-3). Matthew 17:2 and Luke 9:29 make clear that Jesus's face was changed; Mark could be read as suggesting that the Metamorphosis was in the clothing only. For Matthew and Luke, there is a likely allusion to Exodus 34:29b, which describes Moses on his return from Mount Sinai: either his face was shining with rays and so looked glorious or splendid, or his skin became tough, or he somehow grew horns, which were symbols of power (so St. Jerome). Michelangelo's Moses, with horns, follows Jerome's Latin (the Vulgate) reading. I'm inclined to go with shining rays, as if in the encounter with the divine, something of the divine rubs off on us.

For Mark's text, however, we have a focus not on Jesus's face, but on his clothing. A confession: I'm not great with laundry, and I am worse at ironing, but I am aware of how difficult it is to get whites to remain white (I do think of Mark 9 and parallel texts in Matthew and Luke while sorting clothes in the hamper; my husband finds this weird, but he's used to it). In the ancient world, white clothing was unobtainable save for the patrician rich who did not need to venture out into the streets and who had enslaved workers to do the washing. Thus, the white clothing suggests the pinnacle of society.

We can do more than talk about white clothing as a status symbol. For ancient Israel, bleaching is a metaphor, as is washing, for renewal or purification. For example, Jeremiah 2:22 warns, *that if you wash with lye and with much for yourself soap, the stain of your sin is before my face.* Today, the idea of bleaching suggests beautification processes, such as teeth bleaching.

While Mark's statement about white garments can suggest the social elite, it is more likely that Mark is drawing upon the tradition that Adam had glorious garments. Here's another place where historical knowledge may help us better to understand what Mark's first audiences heard. Genesis 3:21 states that God made Adam and Eve *garments of skin.* The Targums, Aramaic paraphrases of this verse, read not *garments of skin* but *garments of glory.* Genesis Rabbah 20:12 recounts that the scroll of Genesis belonging to Rabbi Meir (late first/early second century CE) read *garments of light.* More, Adam's initial luminescence is, in early Jewish as well as Samaritan sources (the *Memar Marqa*), matched up with Moses's luminescence after he talks with God. Jesus, in his shining garments, takes his place as both a new Adam and a new Moses.

In Mark 9, Moses is not replaced; rather, his role is enhanced. *And appeared to them Elijah with Moses, and they were talking with Jesus* (9:4). Commentators frequently note that the order, first Elijah and then Moses, is unexpected and that perhaps Mark thinks Elijah is more important. Chronologically, Moses precedes Elijah; on the other hand, Mark moves backward from Jesus (who interprets both Moses and Elijah in his interpretation of Torah) to Elijah (who interprets Torah) to Moses. Both ancient figures are important. That Moses for Mark represents Torah, and that Elijah represents the Prophets is possible, but for Elijah the claim is a stretch. Mark has cited Isaiah by name, so Mark knows that Elijah does not summarize the Nevi'im, the prophetic canon. Something else, aside from connections to two divisions of the Jewish canon, Torah and Prophets, must be going on.

The three men share much in common, aside from being associated with mountains (Sinai and Horeb). First, they are associated with the messianic age: Moses predicts the coming of a prophet like him (Deuteronomy 18:15); according to Malachi, as we have seen, Elijah is the forerunner of the messianic age; Jesus is, as Mark 1:1 reports, and Peter confesses, the Messiah. Second, all three escape the finality of death. Elijah never dies. Second Kings 2:11 reports that a *chariot of fire and horses* parted Elijah from his disciple, Elisha, and *went up Elijah in a storm* [many translations prefer "whirlwind," which makes me think of Dorothy in the *Wizard of Oz*] *into the heavens*. As we have seen, Malachi predicted Elijah's return to announce the messianic age. Deuteronomy 34:6 states that God buried Moses *in the land of Moab, opposite Bet-Peor, and not does a person know his burial place until this day*, but stories of his postmortem conversations with God remained popular. Philo, the first-century Jewish philosopher from Alexandria, speaks of Moses as flying away to heaven (Moses 2.291). Jesus will die and then rise. The three together reinforce the affirmation that death is not the last word.

Amid this profound scene, Peter, again displaying apostolic obtuseness, intervenes: *And answering, Peter says to Jesus, "Rabbi, good it is for us here to be, and we might make three tents, one for you, and one for Moses, and one for Elijah"* (9:5). No question was asked, so no answer was needed. But Peter along with James and John would have had questions. Had I five minutes with Moses, what would I ask? Whether Miriam composed the Song at the Sea (Exodus 15)? How much of the Torah comes from him? For Elijah I'd start with questions about the widow of Zarephath and her son, move to his experience on Mount Horeb, and be sure to ask about that fiery chariot. The disciples had a chance to ask questions but, whether out of respect or more likely fear, they remain silent.

Peter begins by calling Jesus "rabbi": ironically, the earliest literary reference to someone as "rabbi" comes from the New Testament. Mark does not translate the title, which etymologically means "my great one." John 20:16 translates the term "my teacher" and Matthew 20:33, a rewrite of Mark 10:51, offers "lord" (*kyrios*). The term can mean "teacher"; in later rabbinic literature such as the Mishnah and the Talmud, it connotes teachers of Torah. The fluidity of the term suggests, at least to me, that teachers are not necessarily those with formal accreditation or even formal training. Everyone holds the possibility of being a teacher; everyone can also be a student.

> ***Everyone holds the possibility of being a teacher; everyone can also be a student.***

Three other times the disciples address Jesus as "rabbi." In Mark 11:21, Peter says to Jesus, *Rabbi, look! The fig tree that you have cursed is dried up.* Peter at this point has listened to what Jesus has said, but again he does not grasp the event's import (see chapter 4). In Mark 10:51, a blind man in Jericho responds to Jesus's question, *What to you do you wish I should do?* with *Rabbouni, so that I might receive sight.* Finally, in Mark 14:45, Judas, in betraying Jesus, calls him *Rabbi* and kisses him. Titles, as we've seen, can be misleading.

Peter's suggestion regarding building tents is hospitable and practical but not the best idea for the moment. Suggestions that he is evoking Israel's dwelling in booths during the wilderness period, or that the three tents are related to the wilderness tabernacle, or that they evoke the pilgrimage festival of Sukkot (Booths) don't do much for me. Sometimes a tent is just a tent. And sometimes a suggestion made in the face of something astounding falls flat. Moses, Elijah, and Jesus do not need tents on a mountain; they are not going to remain there in conversation, and they are not staying for lunch.

Mark makes it clear that Peter's suggestion is not on point: *For not did he know what to answer, for they were afraid* (9:6). Indeed.

The expression *not knowing what to answer* reappears in Mark 14:40, another connection of the Metamorphosis to Gethsemane. It occurs the second time the disciples fall asleep and again fail to keep watch with Jesus as he prays. In retrospect, Peter, James, and John might have done well to pray on Metamorphosis Mountain. As for the notice that the disciples were afraid, that motif repeats in Mark 16:8, the Gospel's last line (aside from the appendix). The women flee from the empty tomb, because they were afraid. The men see Jesus in his Adamic glory along with Moses and Elijah—fear is an appropriate response. The women find an empty tomb. But in both cases we know, because we have the letters of Paul, the other Gospels, and two-thousand-plus years of church history, that fear yielded to faith and then action. We know that the women eventually conveyed the message; we know that the disciples, or at least some of them, believed the women.

Mark next tells us that *there was a cloud overshadowing them* (9:7): which "them"? All six? Does it matter? Clouds appear on mountain-tops, including Mount Sinai (see Exodus 19:9, where God says to Moses, *Look, I am going to come to you in a cloud*). Numerous biblical references to clouds, especially clouds that "overshadow," remind me less of trying to discern shapes (it looks like a whale; it looks like the Pillsbury Dough Boy) and more of dense fogs, especially when I walk the dog early in the morning. There's something magical about such times—what had been so clear the day before is now invisible; there is a feeling of moisture in the air, but it is not raining; sunlight is diffused. The cloud forces us to see the world otherwise; it heightens our attention.

And there was a voice out of the cloud, "This one is my Son, the beloved; hear him!" (9:7). The voice, like the cloud, surrounds the men on the mountain. We hear an echo of the baptism in Mark 1:11, *You are my Son, the Beloved*. We remember Moses, who talked about God raising up a prophet like him (Deuteronomy 18:15). Since Jesus does not speak to the disciples on the mountain, the disciples, and we readers, must listen again to the teachings Jesus has already offered, especially his Passion predictions, and we must listen more closely to his words in the next eight chapters.

The scene ends, abruptly, *suddenly, when they looked around, no one did they see but Jesus, alone with them* (9:8). Moses and Elijah will now be understood through Jesus's teachings; they have endorsed his role and, I like to think, encouraged him as he now turns toward the cross. The voice commanded the disciples to listen to Jesus: *Jesus commanded them that no one what they had seen to tell, until when the Son of Humanity out of the dead had risen* (9:9). How frustrating that must have been: they know, but they cannot tell. At the tomb, the women know as well, and do not tell, at least not in the pages of the Gospel. Silence is sometimes warranted, or demanded; sometimes it cannot be avoided, and sometimes silence is death.

The command to silence here fits Mark's Christology, or the understanding of who Jesus is, for to understand Jesus apart from the cross is to misunderstand the gospel. The disciples, who resist the idea that Jesus will suffer and die, can only wonder: *seeking together what it is from the dead to rise* (9:10). It's a good question. There were options: in the body in which one died, in a new body having nothing to do with the corpse in the grave, as a disembodied spirit? How would these risen bodies appear? What could they do, or not do?

In Mark 2:10, Jesus states that *the Son of Humanity has authority to forgive sins upon the earth.* Since his mission, as we saw in Mark 1, is to exhort people to repent because the kingdom of God is drawing near, it makes good sense that this repentance would be connected to forgiveness.

The title "Son of God," which may appear in Mark 1:1, is not how Jesus speaks of himself. He calls himself *Son of Humanity* or "Son of Man" (the Greek is *anthrōpos*). I'm opting here for the more inclusive translation, since a number of my students find the use of "man" as a generic for "humanity" a problem, given that the term has been and can be used to exclude women. On the other hand, I am opting on "son" rather than "child"; while *anthrōpos* can be inclusive of all people, the term translated "son," Greek *huios*, is not inclusive.

As with the "good news," Mark also gradually reveals Jesus's identity. The *unclean spirits* know he is the *Son of God* (5:7); the high priest asks him, *"Are you the Christ, the Son of the Blessed?* (14:61); the centurion at the cross identifies Jesus as *a* [not "the"] *son of God* (15:39). That demons know his identity suggests that acknowledging Jesus's divine sonship is insufficient. As James 2:19 puts it, *You believe that one is the God; well you do. Even the demons believe, and tremble.* The next line insists, *The faith without the works useless is.* Without action demonstrating the belief, proclaiming Jesus is Lord is worse than inaction; it makes the confession not only useless, but also hypocritical.

"Son of Humanity" does more than connect Jesus with other human beings. It can also connote a redeemer figure, as in Daniel 7:13, where one *like a son of a human being* receives power and dominion from God. We do not know what Daniel's first readers made of this odd reference. Likely some thought of the angel Michael, because angels look "like" people.

> **The Aramaic idiom "Son of Humanity" can also mean "one" or "I" as in "one wrote a great book on the Gospel of Mark." The expression is a perfect self-designation for Jesus, especially for the Jesus of Mark's Gospel.**

The Aramaic idiom "Son of Humanity" can also mean "one" or "I" as in "one wrote a great book on the Gospel of Mark." The expression is a perfect self-designation for Jesus, especially for the Jesus of Mark's Gospel. By referring to himself as "Son of Humanity" Jesus asks his followers, then and now, "Who do you say that I am?" Is Jesus human, or divine, or both? More, Jesus does not say he is "like" a "Son of Humanity"; he *is* a Son of Humanity.

Granting the supernatural and salvific aspects of "Son of Humanity" especially in light of Daniel's wording, I prefer the focus for Jesus's self-identification on the human, and so the frail and fallible. This is not to deny the higher points of Mark's Christology: only Jesus receives the commission at the River Jordan; only a divine being can walk on water. But I find that often my students go right to Jesus as the part of the Trinity and so overlook his humanity. We all make mistakes; we all sin by commission (what we do) and omission (what we fail to do). Jesus sees himself as calling sinners to repent. That sounds great in the abstract—I'm all for sinners repenting, and it is much easier to enjoin others to repent than to do it ourselves. Repentance isn't easy. I'd like to think that Jesus, the human being, understands this difficulty as well.

As we move through the Gospel, which now drives toward the Passion, Jesus, once clad in the garments of Adam, will find his clothes divided by gambling soldiers. Jesus, seen in his Adamic glory, is reduced to a naked, tortured, corpse. In 2 Corinthians 3:18, Paul suggests that the transformed body of the Christ is the model and the hope for his followers. Here is the King James Version: "But we all, with open [lit. "uncovered"] face beholding as in a glass the glory of the Lord, are changed [Greek: the verb *metamorphoō*] into the same image from glory to glory, *even* as by the Spirit of the Lord." The image is uncanny, difficult to grasp, but as if through an early morning fog, we can feel it and even see it.

Help My Unbelief (Mark 9:14-29)

Descending from the mountain, the disciples, implicitly invoking the last words of the prophet Malachi and explicitly citing the scribes, question Jesus about why Elijah is to precede the messianic age. Jesus tells them that Elijah has come, but his reference is not to the conversation he had with Elijah on the mountain; it is to the

Baptizer, who in Mark's narrative, as we have seen, takes the role of Elijah (John 1:21 offers a different view). Jesus now makes another Passion prediction, this one based on Scripture: *It is written that the Son of Humanity will experience much suffering and be despised* (Mark 9:12). He is, as we see at the end of this chapter, alluding to Isaiah's suffering servant or slave.

The next scene, the one to which we turn our attention, is called the "Exorcism of the Young Boy" or the "Healing of the Boy with the Spirit." It might better be called the "Challenge of Faith" or even the "Ability to Admit Doubt." Faith and doubt are not mutually exclusive. Faith that does not allow itself to be challenged, faith that does not allow and, better, generate questions, denies the intellect and so part of what makes us human beings. It also threatens to collapse rather than expand.

This is Mark 9:14-27:

And coming to the disciples, they saw a great crowd around them, and scribes arguing with them. And immediately, all the crowd, seeing him, were alarmed, and running out they were greeting him.

And he asked them, "Why are you arguing with them?"

And answering him, one of the crowd, "Teacher, I brought my son to you; he has a spirit of non-speaking. And whenever it overtakes him, it tears him; and he foams and grinds the teeth and dries up [probably: becomes rigid]. *And I said to your disciples that they might cast it out, and not were they strong* [i.e., enough].*"*

And answering them he said, "O faithless generation. Until when to you must I be? Until when shall I endure you? Bring him to me."

And they brought him to him. And seeing him, the spirit immediately convulsed him, and falling upon the ground, he rolled about, foaming.

And he [Jesus] asked his father, "How much time has this been happening to him?"

And he [the father] said, "From childhood. And many times into the fire it has thrown him, and into water, so that it might destroy him. But, if you are able, anything, help us, having compassion on us."

And Jesus said to him, "If you are able—all things are able for the one who believes [has faith; trusts]."

Immediately crying out, the father of the child said, "I believe [have faith, trust]. Help my unbelief!"

And seeing, Jesus, that was gathering rapidly the crowd, rebuked the unclean spirit, saying to it, the speechless and deaf spirit, "I command you, go out of him, and never again enter him!"

And crying out and much convulsing him, it came out, and he [the boy] was as dead, so that many said that he died.

And Jesus, seizing his hand, raised him, and he stood.

The crowds, invested in Jesus's ability to heal bodies and exorcise demons, turn our attention from predictions of the Son of Humanity's suffering to a specific example of human suffering. When I think of the boy's father, I also think about how Mark depicts God (the Father). The God of Israel suffers when people, all in the divine image and likeness, are besieged by demons. I picture the God who mourns by ripping the Temple veil when Jesus dies, as Jews traditionally rip a piece of clothing when in mourning (see Genesis 37:34 for the beginning of the custom).

While several translations attempt to mitigate the crowd's reaction in Mark 9:15 by suggesting that the people were "overcome with awe" (NRSVue) or "overwhelmed with wonder" (NIV) or even "greatly amazed" (KJV), Mark states that they *were alarmed*. The same verb appears three other times in Mark's Gospel, and those other appearances help nuance our text.

According to Mark 14:33, Jesus brings Peter, James, and John with him to Gethsemane, and there he becomes alarmed, or in the NRSVue, "distressed." He is about to be arrested, suffer, be despised, and die. "Overcome with awe" does not grasp the extent of his emotions; "alarmed" does. We should hear those alarms, those sirens. The crowd in Mark 9 is also alarmed: the disciples have failed to exorcise the demon, the boy is suffering, and they do not know how Jesus will react.

The next two uses of the verb appear in Mark's last chapter, the story of the empty tomb. Mark 16:5 reports that the three women who go to the tomb to anoint Jesus's corpse find instead a young man in a white robe, and they *were alarmed*. Of course, they were alarmed: the body is missing! The young man at the tomb, who is probably an angel (and angelic appearances can also produce fear) tells them, *Do not be alarmed* (16:6), and then he shows them the place where the body had been. All four uses of the term, in Mark 9, 14, and 16, suggest times when trust is challenged and fear is present. The crowd fears that Jesus cannot defeat the evil spirit since his disciples have failed. In Gethsemane Jesus faces the challenge of suffering and death. Were he not fearful—were he not alarmed—he would not be human. The women are faced with an empty tomb; the one whom they loved is gone. Of course they are alarmed.

> **Doubt is often a very good thing, as is asking questions when we do not understand.**

All four uses of the term also suggest that faith or trust or belief (the Greek noun *pistis* means all three) need not be perfect. To doubt is human, and it's also a sign of using one's brains. Doubt is often a very good thing, as is asking questions when we do not understand. Had I not doubted (the technical term for this is the "hermeneutics of suspicion") what I had read in many books on the New Testament about how bad early Judaism was and how distinct Jesus was from it, I would never have been able better to understand Jesus. Being alarmed is also not a sign of bad faith; it is a natural human reaction. At times, it can launch us into action; we hear the fire alarm, and we move, quickly; we hear the siren of an ambulance or a fire engine, and we get out of the way, quickly. We hear the alarm clock and we (or at least most of us) get up. The alarm brings us to a state of being awake (see Mark 14:34).

Mark suggests to us that despite doubt or alarm, if we are invested in something, that we persevere and act rather than surrender or flee.

Jesus inquires, *Why are you arguing with them?* (9:16). We can guess as to what the scribes and the disciples were discussing: Jesus's identity? The need for Elijah to precede the Messiah? Questions about fasting or handwashing? It is not clear to me that the disciples have the resources to respond to challenges. Young people are particularly good at such challenges: What do you mean you care for the poor when you just bought a yacht? What do you mean we are saved from sin when we sin all the time? Mark encourages asking the hard questions. Bible study should facilitate the beginnings of answers.

Cutting through the tumult, *one of the crowd*, who turns out to be a desperate father, says, *"Teacher, I brought my son to you; he has a spirit of non-speaking. And whenever it overtakes him, it tears him; and he foams and grinds the teeth and dries up. And I said to your disciples that they might cast it out, and not were they able"* (Mark 9:17-18). Despite numerous attempts by commentators to diagnose the boy's condition—neurological, psychological, chemical, selective muteness, autism, epilepsy—Mark's audience would have taken demon-possession seriously. So do many people today. Whatever we determine regarding the diagnosis, Mark, by detailing the symptoms, insists that we pay attention to the suffering both of the child and of his father. The father has already described his son's condition to the disciples; he had likely described them to healers, and physicians, and priests of healing gods such as Isis, Hygieia, Panacea, and Asclepius. When we have medical need, we use any resource we can find. This father does what must be done to help his child. He does what a good parent or guardian does, whether challenging hospital administrators to offer treatment or government officials to provide more funding for group homes or pharmaceutical companies for affordable medication. He must be exhausted, and yet he perseveres.

The father must speak, for this son cannot speak for himself. This father is not the only parent to care for his child. Mark 5 depicts the synagogue ruler, Jairus, who begs Jesus to heal his daughter on the point of death and who, despite the report of her death, perseveres. Mark 7 depicts the Syro-Phoenician woman begging Jesus to perform an exorcism for her daughter. Even when he refers to her and her daughter as "dogs," she perseveres. The passages encourage parents and caregivers that, even when those who have resources will not help, they must persist.

These scenes, and many others, also remind us of how precious children were and are to parents. We see the concern again in Mark 10:13 with parents bringing their children to Jesus so that he might touch them. The infant mortality rate was high (estimates of 20–40 percent of deaths before age six). Commentators who insist that children were regarded as at best marginalized if not as contemptible misunderstand Jewish culture. When Jesus, in Mark 9:36-37, takes a child in his arms and instructs that whoever *receives one of these children in my name receives me*, he is not speaking of receiving "nobodies," the "socially marginal," the "slavish" or "homeless" or "landless" or "everyone's servant." He is speaking of children, so important in the culture that parent after parent and caregiver after caregiver bring children to Jesus to heal or touch or bless. He is speaking of the vulnerable, the dependent, those who cannot speak for themselves, those who cannot survive on their own.

Mark, here in chapter 9, offers a third story about a desperate parent, and when we put the three stories together, we see an increasing hesitancy on Jesus's part to facilitate the cure. On his way to heal Jairus's daughter, Jesus allows himself to be interrupted by a woman suffering hemorrhages. In the time it takes for that cure to be implemented and for Jesus and the woman to talk about it, the daughter dies. Jairus persists, because Jesus encourages him not to fear but to have faith or believe (Mark 5:36). But Jesus offers no such encouragement in Mark 9. Jesus hesitates to exorcise the Syro-Phoenician woman's daughter: he tells her in Mark 7:27, *permit first to be fed the children, for it is not good to take the bread of the children and to the puppies throw.* And yet she perseveres because "not right now" is not the same thing as "never." But there is no such encouragement here in Mark 9. If we read Mark 9 in light of these other stories, we may hear an assent despite an initial negative reaction. I hear a prompt to persist, despite Jesus's initial rejection. And I hear in the father's words to him good news.

Mark 9:19 is, for me, among the more difficult of Jesus's comments: *And answering them he said, "O faithless generation. Until when to you must I be? Until when shall I endure you? Bring him to me."* The father is not "faithless": if he were, he would not still be advocating for his son. The disciples, obtuse as they are, are not faithless; if they were, they'd return to the boats in the Galilee. Consequently, we do well to determine what Jesus, who sounds petulant at best, means.

Commentators often cite Numbers 14:11 and Deuteronomy 32:20, where the idea of a faithless generation surfaces. Numbers 14:11 describes the wilderness generation, fearing the population of the Promised Land, considering stoning Moses and his associates and even contemplating returning to Egypt. God asks Moses how long will the people refuse to believe despite all the signs that God has given them. Deuteronomy 32:20 depicts God's reaction to Israel's idolatry, *They are a perverse generation* and they are *children who do not have loyalty* [LXX: *faithfulness*] *in them.* Moses then intercedes, successfully, on behalf of Israel in one of the Torah's longest prayers. Read in biblical context, accusations of a faithless generation yield to examples of God's loyalty and fidelity.

The God of the Bible is not without emotion: love and anger, compassion and frustration, rejoicing and disappointment. In terms of textual allusion, Jesus is like Moses: first aglow in the encounter with the divine, and then, down the mountain, to the sickness and sadness, muck and mayhem of human life. Elsewhere, Mark allows Jesus to display this range of emotion. For Mark 1:40-45, the story of the man suffering leprosy, some manuscripts say that Jesus was compassionate and others that he was angry. In modern terminology, Jesus needed to vent. Matthew 8:3 and Luke 5:13 do not mention anger; perhaps their copies of Mark only read "compassion" or perhaps they were uncomfortable with the idea of an angry Jesus. I can see why a scribe would change the response from negative to positive; on the other hand, I find attractive the idea that leprosy would anger Jesus. Cancer and heart disease and especially Alzheimer's disease, which is slowly taking my mother-in-law away from my family, anger me, enough to rail.

Mark's "faithless" generation is not limited to the scribes who have a cameo role in this scene, or the local crowd, or just to others who do not respond positively to Jesus's message. The disciples, too, are part of that faithless generation. It turns out, we are all part of faithless generations because we are all part of the human condition. We are also faithful, because as we find in the father's desperate plea, *I believe; help my unbelief* (9:24), faith and lack of faith exist together. When the Bible speaks about faithless generations, it takes a communitarian approach: we are all responsible for each other; the deeds of one or the few impact the many.

Following his unanswered question about how long he can endure being with the crowds, Jesus orders them (the verb is in the plural) to bring the boy to him. *And they brought him to him. And seeing him [Jesus], the spirit immediately convulsed him [the boy], and falling upon the ground, he rolled about, foaming* (9:20). I cannot image how horrible this situation would have been for either child or parent. Yet some parents go through such horrors every day, multiple times.

And he [Jesus] asked his father, "How much time has this been happening to him?" And he said, "From childhood. And many times into the fire it has thrown him, and into water, so that it might destroy him" (9:21-22). Mark lingers more on the child's symptoms than he does on Jesus's torture on the cross. Jesus had a choice; the child does not. Jesus faced physical torture for a day; the child has suffered for years. Jesus knows he will die on a cross; the father does not know if the child will die from the seizure, from fire, or from drowning. Looking at the cross should prompt us to recognize the suffering of others, even of the earth (see Romans 8:21).

Jesus first asked, *Until when to you must I be? Until when shall I endure you?* or, colloquially, "How long do I have to put up with you?" (9:19). Now the question is *How much time has this been happening?* or, colloquially, "How long has this been going on?" We can read the two sentences as making both theological and psychological points. For God, watching human infidelity is like a parent watching a child having seizures. For this particular father, his question is also "How much longer...must I watch my child suffer? How much longer will he, and I, endure failed medical procedures, failed promises of cures, failed help from family and friends who are also exhausted?"

The father pleads, *But, if you are able, anything, help us, having compassion on us* (9:22). He does not know if Jesus is able. His disciples were not strong enough to perform the exorcism. He begs, *help us;* he demands that Jesus have *compassion on us.* He asks not just for the child but for himself, and for any other friend or family member caught up in this healthcare nightmare. He doubts, *if you are able;* he has faith, *help us.*

And Jesus said to him, "If you are able—all things are able for the one who believes" (9:23). Jesus, according to Mark, cannot do all things. In Nazareth, he was *unable* to do mighty works because of the people's unbelief (Mark 6:5). In Mark 10:27, Jesus explains that for human beings *(anthrōpoi),* not all is possible but *for God all things are possible.* In Gethsemane, he prays, that *if it were possible* for *this hour* to pass (Mark 14:35); he then regroups on faith and possibility: *Abba, Father, for you all things are possible; remove this cup from me; yet, not what I want, but what you want* (Mark 14:36). All things are possible for God. For human beings, not all things. For Jesus, a human being, not all things are possible.

Paul is of help here. In his Epistle to the Philippians, written when he was in prison and expecting execution, Paul writes, *All things I am strong by him who makes me able* or, in the more colloquial NRSVue, "I can do all things through him who strengthens me" (Philippians 4:13). The context tells us that the "all things" requires self-assessment: Paul states that he has learned to be satisfied with what he has because he understands through his own experience what is important and so how to cope (Philippians 4:11-12).

Immediately crying out, the father of the child said, "I believe. Help my unbelief!" (9:24). In my view, this is one of the Bible's most profound verses. Unbelief is not a sign of rejection or disloyalty; unbelief is the place where one asks for help. I don't have the emotional capacity to continue another day: help me. I don't have the psychological stamina to face another moment: help me. I don't believe I can finish this paper or pass this exam: help me. The call for help shows that there remains a modicum of belief, if not in the self then in someone else who can help bear or relieve the burden.

And seeing, Jesus, that was gathering rapidly the crowd, rebuked the unclean spirit, saying to it, the speechless and deaf spirit, "I command you, go out of him, and never again enter him!" And crying out and much convulsing him, it came out, and he was as dead, so that many said that he died (Mark 9:25-26).

The surge of the crowd is the prompt for the exorcism. The father has said all that he can. Jesus responds. Commanding the spirit who blocks hearing, he makes his voice heard. With full authority, and full faith (in God? in his role as Son of God? in his knowledge that the house of the strong man is being plundered by one even stronger?) Jesus commands the unclean spirit to vacate. The demon fights back, with the child's body the battlefield between the cosmic forces of life and death, transfiguring and disfiguring. The battle is so fierce that to the crowd, it appeared the child was dead.

And yet, for Mark, death is never the end. *And Jesus, seizing his hand, raised him, and he stood* (9:27). Jesus refuses to let either demons or death have the last word. He grabs the child's hand, as if conveying his own life force into him, and raises him. So, too, God will, according to Mark, raise Jesus. There are times we cannot do for ourselves what we want. We need help. Children need to be fed and to be carried, and diapers need to be changed. I need help with countless things, from figuring out what to do when my computer goes wonky to figuring out how to work the timer on the oven (cooking is not my forte) to figuring out what are the best words to say or actions to take when someone needs comforting, or when someone does something hurtful. My mother-in-law needs help in taking a shower, getting dressed, and sometimes remembering where she is. The demon-possessed child needed help, which his father could not provide. His father needed help, which the disciples could not provide.

> *Jesus refuses to let either demons*
> *or death have the last word.*

The father did exactly the right thing: he asked, he pleaded, he persisted. We may not know what comes at the end, and we may not take accounts of miracles or demon possession or resurrection literally. But we can find help for our unbelief.

The scene should have ended here, with the banishment of the demon and the raising of the child. But no, once again the disciples, bless their hearts, gloss what they witnessed. *And going into a house, his disciples privately were asking him, "Why were we not able to cast it out?" And he said to them, "This kind by nothing is able to come out except in prayer"* (Mark 9:28-29). Jesus does not, at least explicitly, pray before performing the exorcism. As we have seen, he was more petulant than prayerful. Nor did he tell his disciples, when he commissioned them for their evangelizing tour, that they needed to pray before healing or exorcising.

Why prayer here? Perhaps he is reminding them that although they are his agents in proclaiming his gospel, they do not have the powers he has. They are the ones who, as the *Bat Qol* on the mountain commanded, are to listen to Jesus. To be the agent of God does not make one God.

Or perhaps, as the old saying goes, sometimes the answer to the prayer is "no," or, better, "not now." Faith, or belief, or whatever sustains us, nevertheless allows us to continue.

The Third Passion Prediction
(Mark 10:32-34, 45)

For the Son of Humanity did not come to be served but to serve, and to give his soul as a ransom for many.

Mark 10:45

After Peter's correct identification of him as *the Christ* (Mark 8:29), Jesus speaks not in parables or riddles but plainly to the Twelve. *And he began to teach them that it is necessary that the Son of Humanity much to suffer, and to be killed by the elders and the chief priests and the scribes, and to die, and after three days to be raised* (Mark 8:31). Peter refuses to accept this teaching, and Jesus rebukes him (8:33).

Following the exorcism of the demon-possessed boy, Jesus again *was teaching his disciples and he said to them that the Son of Humanity is to be handed over into the hands of human beings, and they will kill him, and being killed, after three days he will be raised* (Mark 9:31). Details increase: Jesus states that he will be handed over (Greek: *paradidōmi*). The term also means "betrayed." The Twelve do not refuse the message, but there is no acceptance either. The disciples *were ignorant concerning the matter and were afraid to ask him* (9:32). They become like the demon-possessed boy. Jesus called Peter "Satan" for refusing to accept the Passion; now the disciples do not speak, as if they have a spirit of muteness. Some things are incomprehensible: what remains vague in pronouncement can only be understood in personal experience.

Even more details about Jesus's fate surface in Mark 10:32-34:

And when they were on the way, going up to Jerusalem, and there was going before them Jesus, and they were marveling, and those who were following were fearing. And taking again the Twelve, he began to them to say what was about to him to befall. "Look, we are going up to Jerusalem, and the Son of Humanity will be handed over to the chief priests and the scribes, and they will condemn him to death, and they will hand him over to the gentiles. And they will mock him and spit on him and whip him and kill, and after three days he will be raised."

We find a division among those in the entourage, from marvel to fear. We learn of the involvement of the Gentiles, which, given the Jerusalem setting, indicates Roman rulers. We hear of mocking and whipping along with death. To this prediction, the disciples respond not with rebuke and not with silence; they respond by jockeying for positions of authority. This is entirely the wrong response.

The better response would have been to ask why. Why is it necessary for Jesus not only to die but also to suffer? Sacrificial animals are not tortured to death; to the contrary, the death is to be as painless as possible. Nor did contemporary Jewish messianic expectations include a suffering, dying, and rising messiah. Mark 10:45 gives a partial explanation. Following instruction on servant leadership and taking the role of the enslaved, Jesus tells his disciples, *For the Son of Humanity did not come to be served but to serve, and to give his soul* [Greek: *psychē*] *as a ransom for many.*

Jesus was crucified, a Roman punishment for the enslaved, for traitors and rebels, and for anyone whom local rulers wanted to kill. It is conceivable that Jesus predicted his death. He knew what happened to John the Baptizer. He knew that gathering crowds would attract the attention of governing authorities. He was heading to Jerusalem, where he planned something: to challenge authority? To proclaim the in-breaking of the kingdom of God? To see himself crowned king? To die as a ransom for many? In Mark's account,

Jesus's entry into the city prompted the people to shout, *Blessed is the coming Kingdom of our father David,* and, following that, he stops activity in the Jerusalem Temple. He deliberately puts his life in danger.

Jesus may have thought of the Jewish martyrs who died for their people and their God. According to 2 Maccabees, a Greek text found in the canons of the Roman Catholic, Anglican/Episcopal, and Eastern Orthodox Churches, the death of martyrs is efficacious. Set during the mid-second century BCE, after the Seleucid (Syrian-Greek) ruler Antiochus IV, together with some upper-class Jewish priests in Jerusalem, outlawed Jewish practices such as male circumcision and dietary regulations, the book recounts the fidelity of Jews who died rather than compromised their beliefs. For example, 2 Maccabees 6:10 records that two women who circumcised their sons were paraded through the streets of Jerusalem *and from their breasts having the infants* and then they were thrown down from the city wall. The next verse mentions people who assembled in caves in order, secretly, to observe the Sabbath, and who allowed themselves to be burned alive rather than fight back on *that most holy day.*

The same chapter reports how an elderly man named Eleazar went to the rack willingly, spitting out the [pig] flesh forced into his mouth (2 Maccabees 6:19). When some, out of pity, urged him to pretend that he was eating pork (2 Maccabees 6:21) so that he would be spared, Eleazar refused: he would not pretend to eat, lest people think that he, a man in his nineties, would practice foreign rites (2 Maccabees 6:24).

Chapter 7 of 2 Maccabees recounts how seven sons of a widowed mother face torture and death for refusing to commit idolatry. The second son, as he dies, tells the king, "You accursed wretch, you dismiss us from this present life, but the King of the universe will raise us up to a renewal of everlasting life, because we have died for his laws" (2 Maccabees 7:9 NRSVue). Jesus, or Mark, or both, may have been influenced by the role of the martyr as "witness" (which is what the Greek word *martyr* means) to God and God's Torah.

An even more likely source for Jesus's suffering and death is Isaiah 52:13–53:12, the fourth of the so-called "Suffering Servant" songs (Isaiah 42:1-4; 49:1-6; 50:4-11; and 52:13–53:12). Who this figure was, or is, or will be, remains debated. Elsewhere, Isaiah speaks of the people Israel as God's servant, as in Isaiah 41:8, *You, Israel, my servant, Jacob, whom I have chosen, the seed of Abraham, whom I love.* Isaiah 44:1 is addressed to *Jacob my servant, Israel whom I have chosen.* Similar addresses appear in Isaiah 44:21; 45:4; and 49:3. In Isaiah 49:5-6, the servant seems to be the prophet himself. Other candidates include Moses, Jeremiah, King Cyrus (called the *messiah* in Isaiah 45:1), and many others. Daniel 12:3 (also 11:33) identifies Isaiah's servant with the Maccabean martyrs.

It is possible that Isaiah saw Israel as suffering when the Babylonians destroyed Solomon's Temple and took much of the population into exile. Isaiah also knew that the people remained faithful to their traditions. When Cyrus of Persia conquered Babylon in 538 BCE and repatriated many of those exiled, along with their children and grandchildren, other nations noticed. In Isaiah's view, those nations, seeing the suffering and then the unexpected return to the homeland, realized the power of Israel's God.

Scholars today debate (okay, we debate pretty much everything) the identity of the servant, whether the servant mentioned in Isaiah 41 and 44 is the same figure as the servant in Isaiah 49 or 52–53, whether the servant is an individual or represents all the people, whether we should speak of a servant or a slave.

We even debate whether Isaiah sees the servant as dying. That the servant was *cut off from the land of the living* (Isaiah 53:8) could be poetic hyperbole. Nor is it clear that the servant was a sacrifice. Isaiah 53:10 is often translated, "When you make his life an offering for sin" (NRSVue), but the Hebrew is uncertain. It would also be weird to see this servant as a sacrifice, given that the servant is by no means unblemished. Unlike an appropriate offering, he is diseased, infirm, and near death.

Isaiah 40–55, likely dating to the Babylonian Exile or its immediate aftermath, is a prophecy of comfort. The prophet tells the people that they are going home, as we saw in Mark's repurposing of Isaiah 40 to refer to John the Baptizer. The followers of Jesus repurposed this ancient text a second time to see their Lord in Isaiah's servant: The servant is mocked as Jesus would be mocked; the servant's suffering is unjust as Jesus would be condemned by false charges; the servant is wounded as Jesus would be wounded by the nails pounded into his flesh.

Isaiah's suffering servant also underlies understandings of Jesus's redemptive death. In 1 Corinthians 15:3-4, Paul reports the tradition he had received, that *Christ died for our sins according to the Scriptures.* Isaiah 53:12 says of this servant, *and he, the sins of many, took.* Additional connections are easy to spot. For example, according to Mark 14:61 (also 15:5), Jesus remained silent in the questioning of the high priest, as Isaiah 53:7 (NRSVue) says of the servant, *He was oppressed and he was humiliated, and not did he open his mouth, like a sheep to the slaughter he was brought, and like a ewe before the face of her shearer is mute, and not did he open his mouth.*

Jews who did not follow Jesus found their own candidates for Isaiah's servant. In a fascinating move, the Aramaic paraphrase of the Prophetic books, *Targum Jonathan,* translates Isaiah 52:13 as *Behold, my servant* and then adds, *the Messiah.* The Messiah, for this text, is not, however, Jesus. He is rather someone who intercedes on behalf of Israel.

Isaiah's servant is not Mark's only way of understanding Jesus's death. In Mark 10:45 (see also Matthew 20:28 and 1 Timothy 2:6), Jesus states that he had come to *give his soul as a ransom for many.* "Ransom" (Greek: *lytron*) meant then what it means today: payment to release someone or something. Release in antiquity could be from slavery, from being held hostage, from kidnapping or being a war-captive, from being condemned to death, etc.

We get a sense of the term's theological potential through its verbal form, for a "ransom" is both what is paid ("the ransom was $100,000") and how it is paid ("I ransomed the dog back for $100,000"). The verbal form (Greek: *lytroō*) means to set free or to redeem. For example, in Luke 24:21, the two on the road to Emmaus say to the (incognito) Jesus, *We had hoped that he was the one to redeem/ransom/set free (lytroō) Israel.*

Now we have problems: Redeem from what? To whom is the ransom paid? The answer to the first question depends on the text. For the two on the Emmaus Road, redemption could be from Roman rule or from earthly life with all its problems. Ephesians 1:7 (see also Colossians 1:14 and Titus 2:14) speaks of *redemption (apo-lytroō) through his blood, the forgiveness of trespasses.*

The Epistle to the Hebrews 9:12 develops this idea of sacrificial purification, with the blood of Jesus granting *eternal redemption.* Jews, pagans, and Samaritans and so early Christians thought of blood as cleaning or purifying, as if it were theological bleach. For a reading of this ransom in relation to sacrifice, 1 Peter 1:18-19 speaks of the congregation as being "ransomed from the futile conduct inherited from your ancestors, not with perishable things like silver and gold, but with the precious blood of Christ" (NRSVue; see also Romans 3:24-25). The dominant New Testament view of the ransom is therefore that the death/blood of Jesus redeems from sin, and by extension the idea of the cross as a sin-offering.

The ransom Jesus pays is then seen as a permanent offering that resets both individual and human history: a grand do-over in which the slate of sins is wiped clean (not that we still use slates, or even blackboard erasers, but you know what I mean). This graciousness should prompt repentance and then righteous action. We can get a sense of this idea in Mark 10:21, where Jesus tells the rich man who *lacks one thing* to *go, sell what is yours, and give to the poor, and you will have treasure in heaven.* Jesus's payment refills the accounts of that treasure in heaven.

The payee of the ransom is undecided. The ransom could be understood as paid to God, who requires some sort of satisfaction for humanity's sins. I'm not happy with this reading; it plays into the stereotype of the Old Testament God of Wrath vs. the New Testament God of Love, a false dichotomy faithful to neither the Bible nor to the Jewish tradition.

Origen, a second-century Christian, posited that the ransom is paid to Satan. In his view, Satan gained control over history, with Adam and Eve bearing the responsibility. Satanic control explains why evil spirits plague humanity. Mark 1:13 notes Satan's tempting Jesus in the wilderness. The interpretation of the parable of the sower describes Satan as snatching the word from those on the path (Mark 4:15). I'd be happier with this interpretation of Mark 10:45 if Mark had included the extended temptation narrative recorded in Matthew 4:8-9 and Luke 4:5-6, where Satan promises Jesus all the kingdoms of the world. If Satan's offer is bona fide, then he has the earth in his grasp, and so the ransom can be seen as buying it back.

Or perhaps the ransom language is a metaphor that should not be pressed into an allegory. It conveys the idea that we, who were imprisoned, have been set free by Jesus's willingness and fidelity to give his life.

I've never been, and never hope to be, held captive and therefore needing someone to pay what I cannot pay in order to free me. I've never been, thank heaven, so overburdened with debt or caught up in the criminal justice system that I needed someone to post bail for me. But when I think about the various descriptions Mark uses for Jesus—sacrifice, ransom, prophet, shepherd, Son of God, Son of Humanity, Messiah, Lord—ransom has a visceral sense of putting things back to right. I understand what it is like to be rescued when I cannot do what needs to be on my own. I have also helped others who cannot help themselves, and I know that, sometimes, I suffer because of it (along the lines of the saying "no good deed goes unpunished"). Experiencing such ransom, of being bailed out, of someone else shouldering the burden, can be a sign of the Kingdom coming in power.

Regarding the "many" who will be ransomed, the term can be read as limiting: "Many of you will pass this course" does not mean everyone will pass. The more generous reading is that the ransom is for all, but not all will accept it. The less generous reading is that Jesus gives his life to ransom only those who worship him as Lord and Savior. The rest can, literally, go to hell. It will be up to his followers to determine if they want to read with generosity. Instructive here is 1 Timothy 2:6, which insists that the Christ "gave himself a ransom for *all*."

The death of Jesus is, for many Christians, a willing self-sacrifice that redeems the world (or at least many in it, then and now). Dying as a ransom makes meaning out of a torture and murder, and so threatens to justify both torture and murder. In speaking of this ransom, we do well to focus on the *response* to it, good deeds prompted by having a clean slate, with the "debt" of sin paid off. Or, to use the more updated terminology, we've been bailed out. The task now is not to bail on showing appropriate gratitude.

CHAPTER 4

Fig Trees and Tenants

Mark 11–12

As we move into the Passion Narrative, enigmatic sayings and actions return. Mark shows wisdom in encouraging readers to understand, interpret, and reconsider. While some interpreters regard Mark as inept, I see Mark as deliberately provocative, drawing readers in and then encouraging conversation about and continuity of the stories. In this chapter, we attend to one of Mark's most provocative passages, the cursing of the fig tree, and then to one of Mark's most morally difficult passages, the parable of the wicked tenants. Let the conversations continue!

The Cursing of the Fig Tree (Mark 11:12-21)

Mark 11 opens with Jesus's arranging his entry into Jerusalem and the entry itself. The crowd's reaction, *Hosanna, blessed is the one coming in the name of the Lord. Blessed is the coming Kingdom of our father David* (Mark 11:9-10), is the language of a victory parade with the crowd greeting Jesus the conquering king. This king, however, does little upon entering the city. Mark 11:11 laconically notes, *He went into Jerusalem, into the Temple, and looking around at all, late already being the hour, he went out to Bethany with the Twelve.* The scene suggests to me that Jesus is scouting the location. But Mark's literary art also shines: Mark gives us the start of a story, and then offers another story before the first is complete. We saw similar approaches with the mission of the disciples interrupted by the death of John the Baptizer, as well as the raising of Jairus's daughter interrupted by the healing of the women suffering hemorrhages.

The cursing of the fig tree doubles the technique of narrative framing. On the one hand, the curse is sandwiched between Jesus's first visit to the Temple and his return when he stops all work. On the other hand, we can, and do in this chapter, see that second visit as framed by the cursing of the tree and Peter's observation that the tree has withered.

This fig tree incident is not one of my favorite Gospel stories. I am not a fan of ecological degradation, of cursing trees, let alone of killing them. Even if we take the story as a parable about the destruction of the Temple by the Romans, I still don't like it. But I am intrigued by it.

Here's the text, starting with Mark 11:12. I include the Temple scene, but our conversation will focus on the tree. Our text is Mark 11:12-21; in the second section of this chapter, we'll look at its continuation, Mark 11:22-25.

> *And in the morning, when they went out from Bethany, he was hungry. And seeing a fig tree, from a distance, having leaves, he went, if, therefore, something he would find in it. And coming to it, nothing he found except leaves, for it was not the appropriate time [kairos] of figs. And answering, he said to it, "No longer into eternity from you no one fruit might eat." And were hearing his disciples.*

> *And he comes into Jerusalem. And going into the Temple, he began to cast out the ones selling and the ones buying in the Temple, and the tables of the moneychangers and the seats of the sellers of the pigeons he overthrew. And not was he allowing so that someone might carry a vessel through the Temple. And he was teaching, and he was saying to them, "Is it not written that 'My house, a house of prayer will be called, to all the nations, but you have made it a cave of robbers?'" And having heard, the chief priests and the scribes, even seeking how him they might kill, were afraid of him, for all the crowd was astonished at his teaching.*

And when evening was, they were going out of the city. And passing by, in the morning, they saw the fig tree, withered from roots. And remembering, Peter says to him, "Rabbi, see, the fig tree that you cursed, is withered."

I do like the first verse, *when they went out from Bethany, he was hungry.* Did he miss breakfast? Even Jesus needs to eat. Unlike Matthew and Luke, who describe Jesus fasting forty days during Satan's temptation in the wilderness, Mark (1:13) notes only that he was tempted, and that the angels served him. Mark's notice (11:12) that Jesus was hungry reminds us of his humanity. When I am hungry, I get cranky. So do babies, children, teenagers, and pretty much everyone else. And when I expect there to be food, whether bagels in the fridge or coffee in the pantry, and there is none, I am even crankier, especially early in the morning.

Commentators are quick to insist that Jesus, rather than being angry with the tree, used the situation as an opportunity for a prophetic sign. The two points are not mutually exclusive. The man who asks a desperate father, *Until when to you must I be? Until when shall I endure you?* (Mark 9:19) or "How long must I put up with you?" is the same man who loses patience with the tree. Mark forces on the reader the full humanity of Jesus, for better or worse. In him we can find images of ourselves, for better or worse.

> *Mark forces on the reader the full humanity of Jesus, for better or worse. In him we can find images of ourselves, for better or worse.*

We can extend the point: don't curse what cannot be. Indeed, don't curse. Not only will cursing the fig tree fail to provide fruit, it will also prevent the tree (or whatever or whomever) from supporting anyone else. Cursing leads to destruction. When I find myself about to say, "Damn it" (I have those moments), I think about the poor fig tree, and (usually) hold my tongue.

Jesus, who fed five thousand and then four thousand, is hungry. Had he wished to make fruit appear on the tree, that should have been within his capabilities. That he does not make the food appear miraculously suggests to me that something else is going on. Mark makes us wait for full understanding.

And seeing a fig tree, from a distance, having leaves, he went, if, therefore, something he will find in it. And coming to it, nothing he found except leaves, for it was not the appropriate time [kairos] *of figs* (Mark 11:13). He sees leaves and seeks fruit. That he finds none should not be surprising, since it was not the *kairos*—the right season, the opportune time—for the tree to produce fruit. He had hopes, and nature thwarted those hopes. The fig tree does not change its nature when it sees him. It remains what it had always been, a tree that operates according to the seasons, the way all trees operate.

Now comes the very strange part: *And answering, he said to it, "No longer into eternity from you no one fruit might eat." And were hearing his disciples* (11:14). Following the Temple incident, Mark records, *And passing by, in the morning, they saw the fig tree, withered from roots. And remembering, Peter says to him, "Rabbi, see, the fig tree that you cursed, is withered"* (11:20-21).

I struggle with this text. I am not alone. Matthew and Luke did not know what to do with it either. In Matthew 21:18-19, Jesus curses the tree, and it immediately drops dead. Nothing about it being the wrong season for figs. Matthew's message is another indication of Jesus's control over nature such as stilling storms and walking on water. Luke 19:45-48 reformulates the saying into a parable about an unproductive tree. When a landowner orders the gardener to chop the tree down, the gardener responds that he will try fertilizer, and if it still bears no fruit, then the owner can chop it down himself. That's a good message about caring for nature, and for people.

Biblical scholars (including me) love to look for earlier images that might help us interpret later texts, and Israel's Scriptures do contain passages that use unfruitful plants to represent unproductive lives. Isaiah 5, the famous parable of the vineyard to which we shall return in discussing the parable of the wicked tenants, describes a cultivated vineyard that produced only wild grapes. The result: God forbids both human intervention with prunes and hoes and natural help such as rain. The vineyard thus becomes a wasteland (see Isaiah 5:6; see also Ezekiel 19:10-14).

There are twenty or so other references to fig trees: trees in bloom, trees dried up, sweet fruit, no fruit. For example, Micah 7:1-2 laments that after the summer harvest, there is no fig left to eat, and moves to the allegory: there is no one left in the land who is righteous. But if Mark's point is that there are no faithful ones left in Jerusalem, the story of the fig tree doesn't get me there. Other possible connections include Isaiah 28:3-4 (on eating the first ripe fig before summer), Jeremiah 8:13 (the lack of figs on the tree indicating Israel's failures in fidelity), Hosea 9:10 (on the potential of the first fruits of the fig tree), and Joel 1:7 (the splintering of the fig tree as the result of war). On the other hand, Zechariah 3:10 anticipates the messianic age when "you shall invite each other to come under your vine and fig tree" (NRSVue). So far, my search for an earlier text is, well, fruitless.

Nor do rabbinic texts offer much help. According to the Babylonian Talmud (Ta'anit 24a), a rabbi had hired laborers to work in his vineyard (a common motif for parables, as we'll see when we get to the wicked tenants); however, he failed to bring them food. The laborers complain to the rabbi's son that they are starving, at which point the son says to the fig tree, "Fig tree, fig tree, yield your fruits, so that my father's workers may eat." It does, and they do. Good story, but not much help with Mark.

The fig tree is, at least for Mark, just a fig tree; its import is less the fig than the curse. Had the tree been a pear tree or a cherry tree, we'd probably get the same message.

Given the sandwiching (intercalation) of the Temple incident between the cursing and the withering of the tree, we can read the scene as a parable of judgment on the Temple. The tree/the Temple, in this configuration, operate according to their nature. Jesus had hoped that, with his presence in Jerusalem, the Temple would change its nature, from sin to sanctity, corruption to compassion. But the Temple Herod remodeled remained true to its original nature; it did not bear fruit when Jesus appeared. Therefore, both Temple and tree are rotten, cursed, and both will be destroyed. The "not the season" part is Mark's way of speaking of the delay between Jesus's stopping work in the Temple, sometime in the 30s, and the destruction of the Temple by the Romans in 70.

I think this is more or less what Mark had in mind, and I don't like it. (There are other passages in both Testaments I don't like, and when I don't like a text, I wrestle with it.)

Historically speaking, nothing suggests that the Temple itself was corrupt. As we've seen, Jesus's followers continued to pray in the Temple, and Paul sanctions Temple worship. The well-known expression "den of thieves" or "cave of robbers" (Mark 11:17, quoting Jeremiah 7:11) does not indicate a place where people steal; the cave is where robbers go, after they steal, to stash their loot. Jeremiah railed against people who took worship as perfunctory: say the prayer; make an offering; *fail* to repent. Nor is there anything corrupt about the fig tree. The analogy doesn't quite work.

Some commentators see the story of the fig tree as Mark's way of encouraging readers to pray for the destruction of the Temple or, if it is already destroyed, to rejoice rather than lament over its destruction. The idea of rejoicing over the destruction of a place of worship—of the Jerusalem Temple, the Cathedral of Reims in WWI, London's St. Paul's and Nagasaki's Urakami Cathedral in WWII, Birmingham's Sixteenth Street Baptist Church in 1963, the Church of St Gregory in Vinnytsi in 2022 (2022!)—seems perverse to me.

A few commentators go further than taking the tree as symbolizing the Temple. They see the tree as representing the Jewish people, corrupt from the get-go, unwilling to change their nature in the presence of Jesus, and destined to be replaced by the church. I'm even less happy with this reading. Paul states in Romans 11:28-29 that the Jewish people *are beloved, for the sake of their ancestors, for without regret/irrevocable are the gifts* [Greek: *charismata*] *and the calling of God.* Readings concluding that the people Israel are by their very nature corrupt ignore the covenants God made with Abraham and Moses and David, ignore the fidelity of the Jews to this day, and put God in the position of revoking promises.

It may be that Mark intends us to read forward from chapter 11 to chapter 13, where in 13:28 Jesus teaches, *From the fig tree learn the parable. When already its branch soft becomes and it puts out its leaves, you know that near the summer is.* The passage concerns the nearness of the return of the Jesus. The cursing of the tree is thus a warning: the foliage is already present; the *kairos*, the fated time, is near, repent before it is too late. More, you will know that the Temple will be destroyed (it likely already was when Mark wrote the Gospel). Mark confirms this claim in 13:2, where Jesus predicts that not one stone will be left upon another.

At the end, and I've been working on this scene for decades, I am left with the conclusion that the cursing of the fig tree is a prediction of the end of the Temple, understood as doomed for failing to bear fruit.

Here's what bothers me about this reading: It suggests that destruction is prompted by sin. A hurricane in Florida, the bombing of Mariupol, earthquakes in Turkey, floods in Afghanistan, Covid. These must be because of sin. Such comments suggest that dying from anything other than old age is the result of sin, and conversely, good health and long life are indicative of righteousness. No floods in Washington, DC or Moscow—must be lots of righteous people there. Such readings are at best theologically simplistic.

My neighbor in Nashville years ago planted a fig tree (he had to tell me what kind of tree it was; horticulture is not my strong suit either). Each time I see it, I think about this parable. Each spring, the leaves suggest to me not only the fruit that will soon be produced, I am also reminded that not all trees survive the winter, that not all plants find themselves in good soil or have gardeners who understand the importance of mulch, and that cursing the tree—or anything else—rather than taking action for improvement, only leads to frustration.

The Power of Prayer (Mark 11:22-25)

Mark then moves the discussion to the power of prayer, and I find myself still wrestling with this story. I'm not happy about the dead tree, and I'm not happy about where the conversation is going. Mark makes me wrestle again with the text.

The disciples note the dead tree and here is Jesus's response, in Mark 11:22-25:

> And answering, Jesus says to them, "Have faith of God. Amen, I say to you, that whoever, if he might say to this mountain, 'Be taken up and cast into the sea,' and not doubt in his heart but might believe that what is said might be, it will be to him.

> "On account of this, I say to you, all for what you pray and ask, believe that you have received, and it will be to you. And whenever you stand, praying, forgive (let go) if something you have against someone, so that even your Father the one in the heavens, may forgive (let go) to you your transgressions. [But if you do not forgive, neither will your Father who is in the heavens forgive your trespasses.]"

This mountain is, given where Jesus and the disciples are standing, Mount Zion, the Temple Mount. Jesus seems to be advising the disciples to pray for its destruction. This approach is also not helpful. To pray to end evil action is fine; to pray for the destruction of the site of the action (be it property or a person) is not. According to the Babylonian Talmud, Berakhot 10a, Rabbi Meir (late first/early second century) prayed that some gangsters in his neighborhood would die.

His wife, Beruriah (the Talmud acknowledges a number of her legal rulings), berates him, and here I paraphrase: "Are you commenting on Psalm 104:35a, which you are reading as 'Let sinners be consumed from the earth, and let the wicked be no more'?" Are you thinking the verse uses the term *hoteim* ('sinners')? No, the term should be read as *hata'im*, 'sins.' Therefore you should pray for the destruction of sin, not sinners. The argument is, sadly, not grammatically or lexically correct, but if we take it as an interpretation, a deeper meaning, it works.

We have already seen the idea that prayer asked with perfect faith will be granted and have discussed how the claim does not work. I like to think that Jesus is teasing in saying, w*hoever, if he might say to this mountain, "Be taken up and cast into the sea," and not doubt in his heart but might believe that what is said might be, it will be to him* (Mark 11:23). I can picture him speaking with a smile on his lips and a twinkle in his eye. Who can have "perfect faith," not a smidgen of doubt, that prayer will make a mountain move? If there's no doubt, there's no humanity.

Prayer to heal a child who cannot speak and who engages in self-harm? Absolutely. Prayer to be strengthened at the time of trial? Absolutely. Prayer to comfort mourners or those who are diseased in body or mind? Absolutely. Prayer to tell a mountain to cast itself into the sea? We can do better.

> **Doubt is part of the human condition. That we persevere in the face of doubt is part of the human challenge. In such cases, prayer can help.**

Gosh, Mark, maybe in this roundabout way, you've brought us where we need to be. To curse is to harm, and with that curse no one benefits. To curse is to leave us with nothing. More, we should question not only that for which we pray but also how we pray. We are more like that father who honestly asks for help for his "unbelief"; when we think we have "perfect" faith we are more than likely fooling ourselves. Doubt is part of the human condition. That we persevere in the face of doubt is part of the human challenge. In such cases, prayer can help.

The last verse in our section, *[But if you do not forgive, neither will your Father who is in the heavens forgive your trespasses]* (Mark 11:26), I place in brackets because its manuscript attestation is weak. Most English translations proceed directly from Mark 11:25 to 11:27; Mark 11:26 goes missing. Did we notice? The language sounds very much like the "Our Father" prayer in Matthew 6:9-13 and Luke 11:2-4. What would happen if we returned to the fig tree with this verse in mind? Do we forgive all, or do we let just a few curses stand because they make us feel comfortable? Mark again issues a challenge. Thanks Mark, and thanks Jesus, for making us think about matters we'd rather ignore, or cut out.

> *Thanks Mark, and thanks Jesus, for making us think about matters we'd rather ignore, or cut out.*

The Parable of the Wicked Tenants (Mark 12:1-12)

I am not happy with the fig tree incident. I am not happy with this parable either. Just as the cursing and withering of the fig tree is, in Mark's context, likely at least a judgment on the Temple, so our parable at the beginning of Mark 12 is a judgment on the people who run the Temple, the chief priests and scribes. Criticizing people who hold political power because of either wealth or inheritance (the two often go together) and who use that power to line their pockets or enhance their prestige rather than to help the people they govern is fine. The problem is with how the parable has been interpreted in Christian history.

Caiaphas, the high priest, who serves at the pleasure of the Roman governor (Pilate controlled the office), did what he could to keep the peace. While Jesus was not the only one who rejected his tenure—the writers of the Dead Sea Scrolls rejected the Temple leadership because they did not think the priests put in place first by the Maccabees, then by Herod the Great, and then by Rome, were legitimate—there is no good evidence that Caiaphas was corrupt. Josephus, a priest himself, severely criticized several high priests, but not Caiaphas.

Over time, interpreters understood the parable to be not just about the Temple and/or its caretakers. They saw the parable supporting the claim that the promises to Abraham, Isaac, and Jacob shifted from the Jewish people to the Gentile church. This interpretation, known as replacement theology or hard supersessionism, makes God unfaithful, ignores the sins of the church over the past two millennia, and counters the teachings of Jesus and Paul. We can do better.

Here's the text:

And he began to them in parables to speak: "A vineyard a person [anthrōpos] planted, and he put on a fence, and he dug out a winepress, and he built a tower, and he leased it to tenants, and he went on a journey.

"And he sent to the tenants at the appropriate time [kairos] a slave, so that from the tenants he might receive from the fruits of the vineyard. And taking him, they beat and sent him out, empty.

"And again, he sent to them another slave, and that one they beat on the head and dishonored. And another he sent, and that one they killed, and many others, whom on the hand they beat, and some they were killing.

"Yet one he was having, a son, beloved; he sent him last to them, saying that, 'They will respect my son.' But those tenants, to themselves, said that 'This one is the heir; come, that we might kill him, and ours will be the inheritance.' And taking, they killed him, and they cast him out of the vineyard.

> *"What [therefore] will do the lord* [kyrios] *of the vineyard? He will come, and he will destroy the tenants, and he will give the vineyard to others.*
>
> *"Not this Scripture do you know: 'A stone that rejected the builders; this one has become the head, a corner; by the lord* [kyrios] *became this, and it is a marvel in our eyes'?"*
>
> *And they were seeking to seize him, and they were afraid of the crowd, for they know that against them the parable he said. And they left him and went out.*
>
> Mark 12:1-12

Unlike the fig tree, which the other Gospels either rewrote or ignored, this parable does not appear to have troubled early interpreters. Matthew 21:33-46 and Luke 20:9-19 repeat basically the same text.

Mark's parable functions as a type of allegory. We know this because of its narrative frame. The opening, *And he began to them in parables to speak* (12:1), requires that we identify the "them." To make this identification, we return to Mark 11:27, where the *chief priests, the scribes, and the elders* engage Jesus. These people are in charge of the Temple; they also serve as Judea's representatives to Rome. They are not "religious leaders," since they are not leading something we would call a "religion": they do not set theological teachings, tell synagogues how to function, determine how Scripture is to be understood, or how the Torah is to be put into action. The priests are responsible for keeping the Temple operating; the scribes and the elders have limited local political authority. At the conclusion of the parable, Mark states, *And they were seeking to seize him, and they were afraid of the crowd, for they know that against them the parable he said* (12:12). The chief priests and others recognize themselves as the wicked tenants. Matthew, who typically adds Pharisees to Mark's text, has the tenants represent "chief priests and Pharisees" (Matthew 21:45). Luke 20:19 offers "scribes and chief priests."

The tenants are, for Mark, the chief priest, scribes, and elders. Some commentators extend the identification to anyone who, according to Mark, sought to kill Jesus, including the Pharisees and Herodians (Mark 3:6 also 12:13). Others extend the identification to the people in Jerusalem who demanded that Pilate release Barabbas and send Jesus to the cross (see Mark 15:14). Finally, some suggest that the tenants are all "the Jews." Not all allegorical interpretations are textually faithful; not all are helpful.

Conversely, other commentators see the tenants as the people who controlled the vineyard/Israel: the Babylonians, Persians, Greeks, Hasmonean Jews, Romans... through to the Constantinian Church, the Muslim rulers, the Crusaders, the Ottoman Empire, the British, the current Israeli government. The lesson then is that rulers who fail in righteousness will be replaced. We don't need a parable to tell us that governments, whether righteous or not, will be replaced. That is the way of emperors and kings, presidents and prime ministers.

Better may be the view that we are all tenants, we all fail to yield what we should—good deeds, charitable contributions, whatever—to God, and therefore we risk our own security. And yet, we don't need a parable to tell us this either. Again, Mark is making us work, and so we return to the beginning of this parable.

At the start of the story, the owner is conscientious: *A vineyard a person planted, and he put on a fence, and he dug out a winepress, and he built a tower, and he leased it to tenants* (12:1). The owner resembles God in Isaiah's parable: Isaiah 5:1-2 locates the vineyard on a fertile hill; the land is dug and the stones removed; the vines are cultivated; there is a watchtower and a wine vat. So far, so good. The owner has done what needs to be done.

On the other hand, I doubt that this owner built the fence and the tower or dug the winepress himself: if he's rich enough to own the vineyard, he's rich enough to use hired or enslaved workers for the labor. Moreover, he does what is needed to get the vineyard up and running, and then he leaves. Should we immediately take this landowner as representing God? Do all rich men represent God? Perhaps he is just a rich man, like the "rich young ruler" who was unable to follow Jesus because he was weighed down by his stuff. Did this person build the vineyard as a pet project, get bored with it, and leave? I cannot tell, outside of Mark's narrative context, if I am to sympathize with this (rich) owner, or the (less rich) tenants, or both, or none of them.

The fellow, who is just a person (*anthrōpos*) then *went on a journey*. Allegorical readings immediately understand him to be either God, who seemed absent to the people until Jesus, the beloved Son, appears, or as Jesus himself, whose Parousia (second coming) had been delayed. Other parables also talk about an absent lord/ Lord. For example, Matthew 24:45-51 and Luke 12:42-46 describe a "wicked slave" who, recognizing that the master is delayed in returning home, beats his fellow slaves and gets drunk. Directly from these other parables but indirectly in Mark, we are prompted to ask about the relationship between behavior and oversight. Do we behave better when we know we are being watched? Do we behave unethically when we know we won't get caught?

> **Ideally, we provide good fruits because that is the right thing to do and not out of fear of punishment. If we behave appropriately because we are afraid of hell, we turn God into a bully even as we then find an excuse to bully others.**

By extension, I have been asked on multiple occasions why people would behave morally were there no hell. The question floors me. Ideally, we provide good fruits because that is the right thing to do and not out of fear of punishment. If we behave appropriately because we are afraid of hell, we turn God into a bully even as we then find an excuse to bully others. Children do not develop a moral conscience out of fear; to the contrary, fear motivates them to figure out how to avoid detection or to shift blame to someone else.

The parable continues, *And he sent to the tenants at the appropriate time* [kairos] *a slave, so that from the tenants he might receive from the fruits of the vineyard* (12:2). While the appropriate time means harvest season, the term can function on a theological register: this is a final judgment. It is the time for the tenants to present to the "lord" what they have produced. The fruits demonstrate both good stewardship and the legally required share due to the owner. But the tenants do not respect the owner, his emissaries, their contract, or the appropriate time.

Mistreatment of the enslaved messenger follows immediately: *And taking him, they beat and sent him out, empty* (12:3). Detaching the parable from its narrative context in which the tenants represent the Temple leadership, some recent interpreters see the tenants as dispossessed farmers forced to work as sharecroppers on their own land that upper-class absentee owners appropriated by manipulation of debt. Reading the tenants as engaging in a workers' revolution would be more convincing had the parable (a) mentioned that the tenants were the original owners, (b) indicated that the terms of the contract were unfair, (c) depicted the tenants as starving, suffering, or otherwise oppressed, and (d) shown the tenants as making common cause with the slaves rather than beating and then killing them. Finally, if the parable is about a workers' revolt, no one wins. The tenants lose the land, the landowner loses slaves and son. If the message is, "Do not go to war, or you will lose," this, too, is a failed message. As the people knew from the Maccabean rebellion, not all revolts fail. The parable is not about dispossessed landowners; it's about venal and violent tenants.

As the parable continues, the idea of a revolt against a corrupt, rich, absentee owner appears increasingly less likely. *And again, he sent to them another slave, and that one they beat on the head and dishonored. And another he sent, and that one they killed, and many others, whom on the hand they beat, and some they were killing* (12:4-5). Here we move into the hyperbolic and the problematic, for the owner has no reason to think that, if one slave is abused, others would be treated with kindness. Worse, for this man, enslaved lives are expendable.

The traditional interpretation is that these enslaved individuals are Israel's prophets. While the prophets were often ignored (if they were heeded, we would have fewer prophets and the Bible would be shorter), few were killed. Yet Josephus states in Antiquities 10.37-38 that King Manasseh killed not only the righteous people in Israel but also, especially, prophets, and Mark depicts Antipas's execution of John the Baptizer. These depictions, however, place blame not on the people, but on the king.

At this point in the parable, I want the owner to stop sending enslaved representatives; I want the tenants to stop torturing and killing. The situation reminds me of war: generals keep sending troops, the opponent keeps killing the troops, repeat. What happened to negotiation? What happened to alliances between the enslaved and the tenants? Why not have the generals put their own lives on the line rather than send representatives? Before moving immediately to allegory, can we see in this parable events in our own context and think our way through alternatives other than more death and more destruction?

"Yet one he was having, a son, beloved; he sent him last to them, saying that, 'They will respect my son'" (12:6). Yes, the "beloved son" in Mark's Gospel is Jesus; in Mark 1:11, this is the title conferred on Jesus at the Baptism and again at the Metamorphosis (9:7). The term for "beloved," *agapētos*, comes from *agapē*, a term often associated with divine love. The absurdity of sending the Son (capital S) when the enslaved emissaries are abused only makes sense if we think of all these brutalized messengers as indicative of God's consistent out-reach and, so, mercy. Even here I find myself frustrated: rather than

continually send prophets, only to have them ignored if not worse, I'd prefer a direct divine intervention.

Claims invoking historical credibility rather than parabolic exaggeration to argue that the owner was being logical, that he really did think the tenants would respect the son, fail. An emissary, even if an enslaved emissary, embodied the owner, just as theologically speaking the Son is the representative of the Father. By continuing to send messengers, the owner of the vineyard moves from possible to parable.

Tragedy increases: to lose anonymous troops is bad enough; to send one's own child to death is worse. This son is also any person's child sent into battle or sacrificed for a hopeless cause. We should be concerned about anyone's violent death; we tend to be more concerned if the death is of a family member. The parable personalizes the victim. It also reminds us that, as a culture, we tend to pay more attention to the scions of the rich than to the poor.

> *The parable personalizes the victim. It also reminds us that, as a culture, we tend to pay more attention to the scions of the rich than to the poor.*

The beloved son does not, as far as we know, protest. If we were this son, what would we say? Do we obey orders? Do we challenge them? *Let this cup pass from me?*

But those tenants, to themselves, said that 'This one is the heir; come, that we might kill him, and ours will be the inheritance.' And taking, they killed him, and they cast him out of the vineyard (12:7-8). The tenants' killing the son is planned, not spontaneous. They could have gained possession had the owner stopped sending emissaries and stopped challenging their claim. The scenario also sounds like the plot hatched by Joseph's brothers (Genesis 37:20) to kill him, a plot thwarted when Judah counsels the other brothers that they sell Joseph into slavery instead. The intertextual connection suggests that even after previous violence, someone could have stepped in with an alternative.

For Mark, the executed son is Jesus. It is possible Mark adds the note about casting the body out of the vineyard (the smarter move on the tenants' part would have been to bury the corpse and so claim innocence of the murder) because according to Hebrews 13:12, Jesus, *so that he might make holy through his own blood outside the gate suffered.* Alternatively, Hebrews could be drawing on Mark's Gospel. Arguments that the removal of the body is for matters of ritual purity fail for several reasons, including the earlier killings of the enslaved messengers. The better move is to note the compounded horror: following the murder, the abuse of the corpse. So, I worry again: what happens to the bodies of the victims of murder? What happened to the bodies of the enslaved messengers who were killed? The disciples of John the Baptizer claimed his decapitated body; who claimed the bodies of the men crucified on either side of Jesus?

What [therefore] will do the lord [kyrios] *of the vineyard? He will come, and he will destroy the tenants, and he will give the vineyard to others* (12:9). We now have a new identification of the anthrōpos who did the planting and the leasing: he is the *kyrios,* the "lord" of the vineyard. If the "beloved" son and heir is Jesus, this lord has to be God. This allegorical reading blames the destruction of Jerusalem on the tenants, the chief priests, scribes, and elders, for having killed the heir. For Mark, Rome's burning the Temple, accompanied by starving the population of Jerusalem, murdering thousands, and taking thousands more into slavery, is the result of the killing of Jesus. It's an easy step from here to the charge against Jews of being Christ-killers. This is not a step I want to make.

In turn, the traditional reading of the parable is that the "others" who receive the vineyard are the (Gentile) Christians into whose charge Israel's legacy—theology, Scriptures, the promises, the covenants—passes. The Jews, disinherited from being the people of God, are replaced by Gentile Jesus-followers. I do not want to go here either.

It may help to take a step back from the allegory and see how the parable could otherwise be understood. For example, given the events it recounts, we might ask what the vineyard owner could do? His messengers are dead. His son is dead. To allow these crimes to go unpunished is intolerable, at least to me. But there are other options. The rhetorical question asking what he would do allows us to think about what answers we would give. For example, forgiveness, which Mark accentuates (see especially Mark 11:25, *And whenever you stand praying, forgive, if something you have against someone, so that even your father, the one in the heavens, will forgive you your trespasses*) might even include forgiveness of the tenants, as long as forgiveness does not eliminate their taking responsibility for their actions. While the tenants cannot return to life the people they murdered, they could repent; they could put their efforts toward feeding or housing others. They could do what my friends in Riverbend, guilty of murder, do: try to live a meaningful life under certain constraints.

I doubt I could forgive someone who killed my child. But I know people who have. I do not want to be brought to this test.

As far as the parable goes, nothing ends well. The landowner finally acts, and even more destruction occurs. The tenants learn nothing. There is no encouragement to repent and no possibility of restitution. The system is set up not to reform but to repeat. We have no reason to think that the "others" who receive the vineyard will be any more faithful. As human history shows, there is unlikely to be change.

What now? Replacement theology is unhelpful at best. The allegory creates a group of "Christ-killers," and that is also unhelpful. Looking at a non-allegorical reading, in which we are speaking of human tenants and slaves and owners can be helpful, since now, all the way through, we can fill in the steps that could have been taken to prevent the escalation of violence.

We can also retell the story. An early Christian text called the Shepherd of Hermes (Similitude 5.1.1-8) offers an alternative version of our parable. In this version, a man plants a vineyard and appoints his slave to care for it while he goes on a journey. The slave fenced in the vineyard and then weeded the land. Upon his return, the master not only grants the slave his freedom but also makes the slave co-heir with his son. This version ends with the master sending the (former) slave food, who then distributes it to his fellow slaves. While the best version would have been the freeing of all those enslaved, at least in this version no one loses. Perhaps you might also want to construct new versions of the parable.

Glossing the parable is a composite citation from Psalm 118:22-23 and Daniel 2:44-45, *Not this Scripture do you know: "A stone that rejected the builders; this one has become the head, a corner; by the lord* [kyrios] *became this, and it is a marvel in our eyes"?* Jesus asks, "Do you know this text?" The chief priests and elders should. It is part of the "Hallel Psalms" (Psalms 113–118), recited according to rabbinic sources on the pilgrimage festivals, Pesach ("Passover"), Shavuot ("Weeks"), and Sukkot ("Booths") as well as on Hannukah and Rosh Hodesh ("head of the month," the new moon). Whether these psalms were sung at Passover at the time of Jesus cannot be proven. The citation about the rejected stone becoming the cornerstone that Mark records, a direct quote from the Greek translation rather than the Hebrew original, appears also in Acts 4:11 and 1 Peter 2:7.

If Jesus is the cornerstone, then his teachings can be the final guide for how to read the parable. For example, given the Gospel's critiques of both insiders and outsiders, can we see the parable as a criticism of any institution or population that responds with violence rather than any other option? Can we take the parable as a warning to any who would promote their own benefit through torture and murder that their endeavors will be recognized as illegitimate?

We can read the parable as prompting us, with each step the owner or the tenants take, to ask what other steps could have been taken. We can read the parable as a warning about abuse of authority and the importance of stewardship, for the privilege that comes with official positions is not necessarily permanent. Building our own empires by killing others, literally or figuratively, is not a good business plan.

Finally, can we see the psalm as having multiple references? The stone that the builders rejected—the idea shot down by corporate funders or unimaginative dissertation directors; the individual who is refused ordination because of gender; you can name many others—may turn out to be the cornerstone.

CHAPTER 5

The Little Apocalypse

Mark 13

Mark 13, known as the "little apocalypse" in comparison with the longer apocalypse, the Book of Revelation, details the events related to the Parousia, the "second coming" and the final judgment. The term *apocalypse* comes from the Greek for "to reveal" and the identification of *apocalyptic* as a genre comes from the name of the last book in the Christian Bible, Revelation or, in Greek, *apokalypsis*. It is from Revelation that we get the four horsemen of the apocalypse, 666, the mark of the beast, the whore of Babylon, and several other motifs that have entered popular culture. Compared to the horrors of Revelation, Mark 13 is a walk in the park.

In apocalyptic literature, images require interpretation, and the interpretation needs to speak to current concerns. But while parables, despite their hyperbole, have images from the day-to-day world, of vineyards and farmers, sowers and seeds, apocalyptic images are otherworldly. For example, Mark 13:14 mentions an *abomination of desolation* or a *desolating sacrilege* and Mark 13:26 talks about the Son of Humanity coming on the clouds and gathering his elect.

Jesus's longest speech in the Gospel, Mark 13 provides us with clues concerning the end of the world as we know it, and at the same time refuses to state when this end will come. It depicts the Son of Humanity as the eschatological (the end-time) redeemer and thus necessarily addresses the Parousia or second coming. But no timetable is forthcoming. *That* Jesus will return is not in doubt for Mark, but *when* cannot be answered.

I had not originally planned on dedicating an entire chapter to Mark 13. My friends convinced me otherwise. Those who attend more liberal churches find this material alien if not icky. Those both in more conservative settings and in settings of oppression find it comforting. Personally, I find apocalyptic material fascinating. For readers interested less in the end of the world than in how to make present life more meaningful, apocalyptic can function as a reminder that not all can bear to live in the world as it is. For those who perceive themselves as persecuted, apocalyptic offers the assurance that God is still in control, that their endurance will be rewarded, and that justice will prevail. Apocalyptic not only guarantees a final judgment, it insists that such punishment, which may be another term for vengeance, is to be carried out by God, not by human action.

Signs of the End

Mark 13 opens with the disciples calling attention to the impressive stones of the Temple. *Teacher* (*didaskale*, as in "didactic"), *look*, they say (Mark 13:1). The disciples' impression was on the mark. Herod the Great, the father of Herod Antipas, started extensive renovations of the Temple, so that it was not only a house of prayer for all nations (Mark 11:17), but it was also a tourist attraction. Josephus (War 5.222) asserts that the outward face of the Temple was astoundingly beautiful; covered in gold plates, at sunrise the reflection was like the sun itself. The stones weighed up to three hundred tons.

Jesus counters, *Not will be left here a stone upon a stone; which will not be thrown down* (Mark 13:2). The language of *stone upon a stone* appears in Haggai 2:15 concerning the rebuilding of the Temple following repatriation from Babylonian exile: *Before was placed a stone upon a stone in the Temple of the Lord* [YHWH]. In Mark, Jesus rhetorically undoes the construction.

Jesus's statement in Mark 13:2 is partially correct. The Kotel, or Western Wall, of the Temple remains standing almost two millennia after Rome destroyed the Temple complex in 70 CE. Christians will sometimes refer to the site as the "Wailing Wall," since there Jews lamented the Temple's destruction. *Wailing* aptly described how Jews related to the site for hundreds of years. Christians who controlled Jerusalem from the time of Constantine (fourth century) to the Muslim conquest (seventh century) forbade Jews from entering Jerusalem save for one day a year, the already mentioned ninth of the month of Av (Tisha b'Av), when they were permitted to mourn the loss of the Temple. With the establishment of the state of Israel in 1948, East Jerusalem and so the Temple Mount came under Jordanian control. From 1948 until the Six-Day War of 1967, Jordan barred Jews not only from worshipping at the Temple Mount but also from entering the Old City of Jerusalem, including what had formerly been the Jewish Quarter. Since 1967, these areas are now under Israeli control, while the Temple site remains under Jordanian Muslim jurisdiction. For readers interested in the history of Israel/Palestine, Mark 13 provides one prompt for further study.

In Mark 11:21, Peter says, *Rabbi, look!* in relation to the dead fig tree. The tree is dead; the Temple will soon be destroyed. For Mark, the destruction of the Temple in 70 is not the beginning of the end, although likely a number of people living at the time thought it was. We can ask ourselves: is there any building, any landmark, without which we cannot live? And then we think—given the destructions of 9/11, for example—the answer may be no.

Jesus plausibly predicted the destruction of the Second Temple. The First Temple, whose construction the Bible attributes to King Solomon, was destroyed by the Babylonians in 586 BCE, so the idea of the destruction was not unthinkable. A text we call 11QTemple (11 for the cave number, Q for Qumran, and Temple for the subject matter) or the "Temple Scroll," one of the Dead Sea Scrolls, posits an alternative Temple to the one then in Jerusalem, since the covenanters at Qumran thought, with good reason, that the Jerusalem Temple's high priesthood was illegitimate. Had Jesus made such a prediction, he was not the only one. In War 6.300-9, Josephus describes a fellow named Jesus (the name was not uncommon) son of Ananus who cried out against the Temple: "A voice from the east, a voice from the west, a voice from the four winds, a voice against Jerusalem and the holy house, a voice against the bridegrooms and the brides, and a voice against this whole people!" When local elites arranged for him to be roughed up, he did not stop his cries. Even flogging ordered by the Roman procurator Albinus did not dissuade him from lamenting, "Woe, woe to Jerusalem." Albinus concluded that this Jesus was insane. After seven years and five months of bewailing the destruction of the Temple, this Jesus dies when he is hit by a stone hurled by a Roman siege-engine.

The fact that the Temple was destroyed gives credibility to the rest of Mark 13. Alternatively, Mark, writing after 70, might have placed references to the Temple's destruction on Jesus's lips. The technique of vaticinium ex eventu or prophesy-from-the-event was not uncommon in antiquity. It appears in pagan, Jewish, and Christian writing, and it is especially common in apocalyptic texts. Daniel 7–12 is a premier example. The writer, speaking in the voice of an ancient figure, "predicts" the future. We can often date the text by determining the point at which the recording of what has already happened stops and the author begins to speculate on what will occur. This technique is how biblical scholars date the apocalyptic material in Daniel to the 160s BCE. What comes next in Mark 13 is a combination of past event and future prediction. What we have in Mark 13 are words from Jesus as remembered and, perhaps, embellished by the evangelist.

Peter, John, James, and surprisingly Andrew, who has not been part of the inner circle and who did not witness Jesus's Metamorphosis, then sit with Jesus, opposite the Temple on the Mount of Olives, and ask, *Say to us, when these things will be, and what [will be] the sign when are about to be these things accomplished all?* (Mark 13:4). "Tell us when," the disciples ask. "Tell us what signs to look for." The setting suggests Zechariah 14:4, which predicts the LORD standing on the Mount of Olives to inaugurate the eschaton. On the other hand, that might be where Jesus and his disciples had a conversation.

The rest of the chapter is Jesus's response.

Frustratingly (at least to me), Jesus does not answer the questions they asked. Jesus often responds not to questions asked but rather to refocus the questioner's concerns. This move is consistent with the best of media training. When the press asks, "Will you raise taxes?" savvy politicians pivot to talking about the importance of not wasting tax dollars, assuring the public that special interest groups will not dictate policy, and condemning the pork-belly projects of their opponents. Mark's Jesus is not seeking to escape journalistic traps. He is rather helping disciples both keep their hopes alive and prepare for difficulties until the end-times come.

> **Mark is convinced that Jesus will return to execute a final judgment. Mark is also convinced, and needs to convince readers, that the timing cannot be predicted.**

The timing of the end, of the world as known at the time, remains indeterminate. Mark is convinced that Jesus will return to execute a final judgment. Mark is also convinced, and needs to convince readers, that the timing cannot be predicted. Such need continues: throughout Christian history, individuals have predicted the date of the end, and each time, they have failed. As a few of my more eschatologically oriented students have responded when I point out the 100 percent failure rate, "Mistakes in the past do not mean that my calculation is wrong." So far, they've been wrong. The danger of such predictions is at least twofold. First, it prompts people to give up their jobs or their education, to give everything away since they do not think anything is needed, to remain unconcerned about ecology or economy, voting, or planting crops. Second, when the dates they predict for the return of Jesus come and go, the disappointment is devastating.

For Jesus, the salient question is not the "when" of the end-time, but the "how" of living with this expectation.

His first instruction is to be skeptical of those who claim to speak for him, or as him: *Jesus began to say to them, "See that no one you deceives. Many will come in my name, saying that, 'I am,' and many they will deceive"* (Mark 13:5-6). He repeats this warning in 13:21-22, *"And then if someone to you were to say, 'Look! here the Christ!' or 'Look! There!'—do not believe. For will be lifted up false christs and false prophets and they will give signs and omens, to lead astray, if possible, the elect."* The idea that individuals would claim to be Jesus was not beyond belief. Herod Antipas was curious as to whether Jesus was John the Baptizer, whom he had beheaded (Mark 6:14).

False prophets are already a concern in Deuteronomy 13, which warns against those who deceive with "omens or portents" (Deuteronomy 13:1-2) and entice the people to follow other gods. So much for anyone who would proclaim a politician, athlete, singer, pastor, whoever, as divinely appointed. When the Messiah comes, or comes back, there will be no doubt.

Next, Jesus speaks of what have been called the "birth pangs" (Mark 13:8) of the Messiah. The imagery, from pregnancy, indicates that when the pain starts, new life will begin. What is now suffering will turn to joy. The date the labor pains will start cannot be predicted, but given a healthy pregnancy, we know that once the labor pains start, the birth is inevitable. The metaphor is also apt, given that false labor, and false messiahs, are also in view.

For Mark, everything is proceeding according to divine plan. The pangs consist, first, of wars, rumors of wars, earthquakes, and famines. We in the industrialized West see wars, earthquakes, and famines from a distance; for Mark's first readers, they were real-time events. Roman historians record earthquakes in Asia Minor in 61 and in Italy in 63. According to Acts 11:28, a Christian prophet named Agabus predicted a worldwide famine while Claudius was emperor (41–54). The problem for using these events to predict the end-time is that wars and famines and earthquakes continue, across the globe, century by century.

The pangs also concern persecution of Jesus's followers by non-messianic *synagogues* and by *governors and kings* (Mark 13:9), representatives of Rome. Why were they persecuted? Pagans (Gentiles) were expected to worship the local gods, understood to protect their cities; pagans who renounced their own gods to worship the God of Israel were in the eyes of their neighbors and of the state, traitors. Jewish Christ-followers such as Paul, who as an apostle received synagogue discipline (2 Corinthians 11:23-24), put local Jewish communities in danger, for the message demanding that pagans forsake their gods stemmed from Jews. That these followers worshipped a crucified Jew exacerbated the negative impression they made. Local synagogues may have also regarded their proclamation of the Christ as promoting a second God (see Philippians 2:6-11) and therefore as blasphemous.

For followers undergoing persecution, Jesus responds in Mark 13:11b, *Do not worry in advance concerning what you will say, but whatever may be given to you in that hour, this say, for not is it you, the ones speaking, but the Holy Spirit.* The proclamation is thus inspired speech. The point about the Holy Spirit providing voice in difficult circumstances makes good sense: such trials can draw from us reserves of strength and even eloquence that we did not know we possessed.

The proclamation of Jesus as lord was not only, especially in the Gentile world, a political issue, it was also a familial one. To refuse to worship the local gods is also to refuse the beliefs of one's family. Thus, Jesus next speaks about betrayal by family members: *And will hand over brother a brother to death, and father a child, will turn children against parents and put them to death* (Mark 13:12). Shakespeare's "How sharper than a serpent's tooth it is to have a thankless child!" (*King Lear*, Act 1, Scene 4) had nothing on Jesus; more, *King Lear* is fiction; what Mark records happened. It still happens, across the globe, when one family member rejects the convictions of the others.

Mark concludes this first section of chapter 13 with the notice, *You will be hated by all on account of my name, but the one enduring/remaining steadfast to the end, this one will be saved* (Mark 13:13). The horrific prediction is actually a form of assurance. The result of fidelity will first be hatred but will ultimately be salvation (Mark 13:13). When my dentist (I like my dentist) says, "This will hurt a bit, but after that you'll be pain-free," I can better bear the pain since I have been warned. The same point holds for labor: it gets worse before the birth but then, with good care and luck, all is well. Without the warning, the experience of pain is more severe and sometimes unbearable. Things will get worse, much worse, says Mark 13, but endure, for in the end, what you have faced will be worthwhile.

The endurance that Jesus encourages in Mark 13 concerns fidelity in the face of hatred and persecution. He is not suggesting that the end-times are upon us because a barista wished us "Happy Holidays" rather than "Merry Christmas." A skinny vanilla latte in a Happy Holidays cup is not an eschatological sign. We should think rather of people who have been and still are persecuted in parts of the world because they convert to Christianity from the dominant religion, or of people who are persecuted because they practice one type of Christianity—or any other religion—rather than another.

The Impossibility of Predicting the Eschaton (Mark 13:14-23, 32-37)

In Nashville, where I live, signs of the end-time are impossible to miss. Since before Covid struck and continuing through the pandemic, a fellow near a shopping center not too far from my house has been carrying a large sign exhorting drivers to repent because Jesus is returning soon. In early 2011, an organization sent out a "save the date" notice to greater Nashville with billboards announcing that Jesus would return on May 21. He didn't. In December 2022, the Pew Research Center noted that 47 percent of adult Christians in the United States believed that we are living in the end-times, with Black Christians at a high of 76 percent, followed by Evangelical Protestants at 63 percent. Numbers were comparatively higher for people without college degrees and with lower incomes. Many who did not express beliefs that we are in the end-times nevertheless insisted that Jesus will, at some point, return; the numbers are 55 percent for all US adults, with Evangelical Protestants at 92 percent.[1]

> **How does one live with both expectation of the end-times and knowledge that such times may not occur in this generation, or the next, or the next after that?**

Mark Twain attributed to Benjamin Disraeli the phrase, "There are three kinds of lies: lies, damned lies, and statistics." Polls can have confusing wording; results can be interpreted variously. But I do not think the Pew results are off the mark. Nor do I find the belief ridiculous. If one begins with the premise that Jesus is God, then it follows that if he makes a prediction, it will come true. Similarly, Jews have been waiting since before the time of Jesus for the lion to lie down with the lamb, for friendship and not for dinner, and for justice to roll down like water (see Amos 5:24). The eschatological issue is not to predict the when, but to practice the how: How does one live with both expectation of the end-times and knowledge that such times may not occur in this generation, or the next, or the next after that?

---

1   Diamant, Jeff. "About Four-in-ten U.S. Adults Believe Humanity Is 'Living in the End Times'." Pew Research Center, Accessed April 7, 2023. https://www.pewresearch.org/fact-tank/2022/12/08/about-four-in-ten-u-s-adults-believe-humanity-is-living-in-the-end-times/.

Mark 13 is helpful on such questions, since it reassures Jesus's followers that he will return even as it tells them to stop calculating the date. For example, Mark 13:10 insists, *And to all nations first it is necessary to be proclaimed the gospel/good news* [euangelion]. Individual Christians will need to determine whether and to what extent they want to promote this message. In some countries, proselytizing is illegal; should Christians break the local laws to promote the gospel? If Evangelical Protestants want to evangelize in schools and hospitals, should Roman Catholics, Mormons, Muslims, and Wiccans have the same right? Are Jews to be proselytized, or are we already under covenant?

The next predictions are, again, not about when but about how. Attempting to determine the when is not only impossible, it is also is a failure to take Jesus at his word. Here is Mark 13:14-18, 32-33.

> *Whenever you see the detestable thing of desolation standing where it must not be—the one reading must understand—then those in Judea are to flee to the mountains, and the one on the housetop must not go down nor enter to take up anything out of his house. And the one in the field must not turn into back to take up his garment.*

> *And woe to those who in womb are having [are pregnant] and the ones breastfeeding in those days! Pray that it may not be in winter/ bad weather. . . .*

> *But about that day or hour no one knows, not the angels in heaven, not the Son, but only the Father. See, watch, for not do you know when the appointed time* [kairos] *is.*

Apocalyptic literature captures readers' interests by describing mysteries and hinting that select—or better, *elect*—readers have knowledge required to decode those mysteries. Mark has already dropped several hints of having insider knowledge. In 4:11, Jesus tells the disciples that they have the secret of the kingdom of God. In 4:34 the narrator mentions that Jesus spoke to the crowds in parables but explained everything to his disciples in private (although given the disciples' frequent failures, it may be just as well that most of the explanations of parables are not preserved; thus, they are invitations to readers, then and now). Peter, James, and John, and we readers, witness the Metamorphosis. In Mark 13, Jesus again offers teaching that requires special knowledge. When Mark states, *Whenever you see the detestable thing of desolation standing where it must not be—the one reading must understand,* that aside—*Let the reader understand*—means that *detestable thing of desolation* (verse 14), or, more commonly, *abomination of desolation,* refers to something specific.

Since Mark speaks of a "reader" in a cultural context in which most people were illiterate, specialized knowledge is in play. The concern for reading sends us back to the only Scriptures that were to both Jesus and Mark authoritative, the Scriptures of Israel. The phrase *abomination of desolation* appears in Daniel 7–12, another example of apocalyptic literature. While the meaning of the Hebrew of Daniel 9:27 is uncertain, the verse appears to speak of King Antiochus IV Epiphanes, who will cancel all legitimate sacrifices and offerings and set up instead *an abomination that desolates.*

The same phrase appears in Daniel 11:31 and 12:11 as well as in 1 Maccabees 1:54 (see also 2 Maccabees 6:5). Scholars debate what this abomination was: a statue of Zeus or of the Syrian god Baal Shemayin ("ruler of the heavens") or a non-kosher offering. Whatever it was, it was bad. For Daniel, this abomination presaged the eschaton. It did not. According to 1 Maccabees 6:7, the rebels removed this abomination.

For later readers of Daniel, the reference pointed to a future abomination. To understand Mark 13:14, we need to determine what event would be comparable to this earlier desecration. One possibility is the attempt by the Roman Emperor Caligula to place his statue in the Jerusalem Temple around 40 CE. (The Jewish people engaged in a sit-down strike to prevent this desecration from happening, and then Caligula was assassinated.) The problem with this view is that Mark, writing around 70 or later, would have known that the plan failed. Other candidates include the takeover of Jerusalem by Zealot factions during the first revolt and/or their replacement of the Roman-appointed high priest with their own man: Titus, the Roman general (later emperor) who led the siege of the city, the Roman conquest of Jerusalem in 70 and the burning of the Temple. Or, Jesus, or Mark, could have repurposed Daniel's phrase but left its reference vague.

Because "abomination of desolation" is an open term, over the centuries it has been applied to various people and events. The same can be said for the "beast whose number is 666" (Revelation 13:18) once the recognition that the original reference was to the emperor Nero was lost. We can speculate: What would a desolating sacrilege be in modern terms? For example, during WWII, many Christian clergy placed a swastika next to the cross on the altar. For those clergy and many of their parishioners, the union of church and state was patriotic. For others, the swastika on the altar was an abomination. Can we recognize an abomination when we see it?

These verses from Daniel, 1 Maccabees, Mark 13:14, and its parallels in Matthew and Luke, make me vigilant when I enter a house of worship: What are the symbols this building employs? What art decorates the sanctuary? Who is depicted and how? In July of 2022, I attended the Oberammergau Passion Play with several Protestant friends who were involved in translating into German the *Jewish Annotated New Testament,* second edition, which I edited with Marc Brettler. During intermission, we wandered into the local Protestant church, where I saw a stained-glass window depicting the "mockery of Jesus" (see Mark 15:15-20) with stereotypical demonic images of Jews. My German Protestant friends were even more horrified than I. Attempts are now being made to address this window, whether to remove it or to put a statement, and an apology, next to it. When we see an abomination, what do we do with it? The same questions can be and have been raised regarding statues, quotations, names on buildings, and so on.

According to Mark 13, the abomination of desolation functions as a sign that people must stop what they are doing. Mark insists, *then those in Judea are to flee to the mountains. [And] the one on the housetop must not go down nor enter to take up anything out of his house. And the one in the field must not turn into back to take up his garment* (13:14-16).

Whenever this end-time comes, it will be unexpected. The scenario could be a natural disaster, like the second eruption of Vesuvius that caught the residents of Pompeii unaware. The scene recollects the destruction of Sodom and Gomorrah; according to Genesis 19:17, the two angels tell Lot and his family, *Escape upon your soul (i.e., run for your life); do not look behind you and do not stand in all the valley; toward the mountain escape, lest you will be swept away.* The warning Jesus gives in Mark 13 had been issued before; it continues to be issued when a train carrying chemicals wrecks, when rivers overflow their banks, when terrorists plant bombs, when a pandemic hits.

It is often easier to explain disaster as punishment for sin, since divine punishment indicates that whatever happens is just and that God is still in control. In other cases, disaster is the prompt to question belief in a just heavenly power. Mark prompts such questions: When disaster strikes, what theological resources can be adduced? More, what could have been done to prevent the disaster?

Mark's references to the flight may allude to the tradition, recorded by the fourth-century church historian Eusebius in his Ecclesiastical History, that Jesus's followers in Jerusalem fled to the city of Pella, in the Decapolis (where Jesus exorcised the demon-possessed man described in Mark 5:1-20) at the outbreak of the First Revolt. Scholars continue to debate whether Eusebius is recording legend or fact. The story helps us with the question faced by any in a war zone: stay, fight, and possibly die, or flee and (hopefully) live?

Impossibility of predicting the date of the end-time continues: *And woe to those who in womb are having [are pregnant] and the ones nursing in those days!* (13:17). Wars and disasters take a special toll on those who are pregnant and who are nursing infants. I appreciate the attention to wombs and breasts, and I also cannot help today but think of those states that would criminalize doctors who treat ectopic pregnancies or mothers seeking to abort a fetus with catastrophic genetic defects.

Again, no one said this study would be easy. Jesus, as Mark depicts, makes us ask the difficult questions and then provides us the resources for addressing them.

The text continues: *Pray that it may not be in winter/in a storm* (13:18), and I think of issues of climate change. Yes, I am aware that Jesus was not talking about twenty-first-century America. But the warnings in Mark 13 speak to me, nonetheless.

This section of Mark 13 ends with a reiteration of the impossibility of predicting the Parousia, the return of Jesus, *But about that day or hour no one knows, not the angels in heaven, not the Son, but only the Father. See, watch; for not do you know when the appointed time is* (13:32-33). I have had friends tell me that Jesus did not know the day or the hour, but they could predict the week. I'm not convinced.

> **Apocalyptic literature is designed to comfort its readers by assuring them that God is in control of history, that they are privy to mysteries people on the outside will never know, that there will be an end to whatever they find oppresses them, and that their fidelity will be rewarded.**

Apocalyptic literature is designed to comfort its readers by assuring them that God is in control of history, that they are privy to mysteries people on the outside will never know, that there will be an end to whatever they find oppresses them, and that their fidelity will be rewarded. For complacent readers, Mark insists, "Wake up!"

The Return of the Son of Humanity
(Mark 13:24-27)

Those of us who have persevered through the first part of Mark 13 can rejoice at the return of Jesus, here presented as the Son of Humanity (*anthrōpos*):

> But in those days, after that tribulation, even the sun will be darkened, and the moon will not give her light.
>
> And the stars will be out of the heaven falling, and the powers, the ones in the heavens, will be shaken.
>
> And then they will see the Son of Humanity coming in clouds with great power and glory.
>
> And then he will send the angels, and he will gather together [his] elect from the four winds, from the end of the earth to the end of heaven.

Today, the sentence *But in those days, after that tribulation, even the sun will be darkened, and the moon will not give her light* (13:24) is sometimes interpreted as depicting what happens after we almost blow our world into oblivion with atomic weapons. Yet we watch disaster movies in which a comet hits the earth or a chemical agent enters the atmosphere or someone sets off an atomic bomb, and the earth is incased in darkness as people die from, well, pretty much everything. In August 2022, *Parade Magazine* published a list of the 26 best End-of-the-World movies. Do we watch because we are afraid, and at the end of the movie we can feel the relief of having it over?

Revelation 13 gives us an ancient version of such movies. We suffer through the horror, and then we, the elect, survive and thrive in the new creation. Apocalyptic texts thus function in part like disaster movies. They tell us that we can recognize the end-times, tell us what to do in the interim, and assure us that since we have the keys to survival, we will be among the elect and the saved.

We can see the ancient view of science in the phrase *the moon will not give her light*. I've kept the gendered language in this translation. In Greek, nouns can be masculine, feminine, or neuter, and "moon" (*selēnē*) is a feminine noun. Showing that the chapter is a combination of metaphor and vision and speculation, but not science, is the phrasing about the moon not giving her light. While the phrase fits what was considered "science" in antiquity, today we know that the moon is not itself a light source; rather, it reflects the light of the sun.

Nevertheless, people in antiquity did see the sun darkened, whether by clouds or by an eclipse; the moon, too, can be cloaked by clouds or eclipsed by the earth. Ancient people would also be familiar with *the stars will be out of the heaven falling*, as appears to happen during meteor showers. These opening lines resemble the prophecy in Joel 2:30-31 (Hebrew text: 3:3-4), which speaks of heavenly portents, with the sun being turned to darkness and the moon to blood *before comes the day of the Lord* [YHWH], *great and fearsome*. Jesus is not speaking of something unfamiliar. Many people believed the messianic age, the "day of the Lord" that meant the final judgment, would come with such portents (see also Isaiah 13:10-11; Jeremiah 4:23; Ezekiel 32:7-8, and elsewhere; for an alternative New Testament description, see Revelation 6:12-14).

> **The re-creation, under the authority of the Son of Humanity, then becomes the final victory over chaos.**

The scene is also an allusion to Genesis 1 for in the apocalyptic worldview, the end of time looks like the beginning of time. In Genesis 1:3, God begins creation by saying, *Let there be light*. At the end of time the light fails. In Genesis 1:4, God separated the light from the darkness. At the end of time, the darkness returns, and the separation is removed. To re-create thus requires un-creation. The re-creation, under the authority of the Son of Humanity, then becomes the final victory over chaos.

The next line, *and the powers, the ones in the heavens, will be shaken* (13:25b) refers to various heavenly beings, such as angels, but not only them. Even in Jewish thought, the idea that the sun, moon, stars, and planets were sentient prevailed. Romans 8:38 speaks of "powers" along with angels and principalities in describing various forces, natural and supernatural, that cannot separate fellow followers of Jesus from the love of God. Colossians 1:16 mentions *the things visible and the things invisible, whether thrones or lordly authorities or principalities or authorities* (see also 1 Peter 3:22) and Ephesians 6:12 mentions struggles not against human ("blood and flesh") forces but against cosmic powers and malevolent forces.

Today, in our post-Enlightenment Western worldview, we separate the divine and the earthly; in antiquity, there was more of a sliding scale. The ancient world was alive with supernatural beings, both benevolent and malevolent. For Mark and for the rest of the New Testament, the Christ, the Son of Humanity, ruled over them all.

His appearance cannot be missed: *And then they will see the Son of Humanity coming in clouds with great power and glory* (13:26). The antecedent of "they" is the powers in heaven, but the reference need not be so limited. As the signs of the end are cosmic, so, too, is the return to earth of the Son of Humanity.

This prediction of what today is known as the Second Coming is repeated In Mark 14:61-62. Caiaphas the high priest asks Jesus, *Are you the Christ, the Son of the Blessed?* Jesus responds, *I am*. The identification, *egō eimi* in Greek, is how God self-identifies to Moses at the burning bush. The Hebrew of Exodus 3:14, sometimes translated "I am that I am," has the connotation of "I will be what I will be"; the Greek reads, *egō eimi ho ōn*, "I am the one being." Jesus then adds, *and you will see the Son of Humanity seated at the right hand of the Power and coming with the clouds of heaven*. While the third-person phrasing could be understood as referring to someone other than himself, nothing in the Gospel, and nothing in my own studies of Jesus of Nazareth, hints that Jesus thought of a second savior other than himself.

The phrase *seated at the right hand* is an allusion to Psalm 110, which had already been mentioned in Mark 12:35-37. Mark reports that when Jesus was teaching in the Temple, after he had parried questions about taxation, marriage in the resurrection, and the Greatest Commandment, Jesus asked a question of his own: *How do they say, the scribes, that the Christ the son of David is?* He then quotes Psalm 110:1, a psalm attributed to David: *David himself said, by the Holy Spirit, "Said the Lord said to my Lord, 'Sit at my right hand.'"* Jesus then concludes his question with the conundrum, *David himself says he is lord, so how is he his son?* The point is that no one would call his child also his "lord."

The question works, but only in Greek translation. The Hebrew of Psalm 110:1 says, "The LORD [*YHWH*] says to my lord [*adoni*]" so that it is clear the first reference is to God and the second is a reference to King David. When the Hebrew is translated into Greek, both *YHWH* and *adoni* are rendered as *kyrios*.

Here in Mark 13, Jesus's statement about the *Son of Humanity coming in clouds with much power and glory* reminds Mark's audience of the conversation in the previous chapter, encourages a return to the Scriptures of Israel to find Jesus's presence (retrospective readings), and assures that, with Jesus enthroned in the heavens, nothing has thwarted the divine plan for history. Thus, despite its detailing of massive destruction, apocalyptic is designed to comfort its "elect" readers.

Whereas some apocalyptic texts revel in the destruction of enemies (e.g., Revelation 19:20's *lake of fire*), the coming of the Son of Humanity in Mark 13 is about gathering, not about retribution. Mark leaves up to the reader's imagination what will happen to those who refuse the message of the Gospel, or those who actively seek to stop it. Just as well. Violence responding to violence does not resolve the problem; no lessons are learned; no transformation is possible.

> **Mark leaves up to the reader's imagination what will happen to those who refuse the message of the Gospel, or those who actively seek to stop it....Violence responding to violence does not resolve the problem; no lessons are learned; no transformation is possible.**

Mark 13 continues with the notice that *he will send the angels, and he will gather together [his] elect from the four winds, from the end of the earth to the end of heaven* (13:27). The idea of gathering the elect suggests that at present the elect are dispersed, and the Greek term for "dispersion" is "diaspora." One eschatological belief, still held by some Jews (and some Christians) today, is that in the messianic age, the Jews dispersed from the land of Israel and living in the Diaspora, whether Egypt or Rome, Asia Minor or North Africa, or, for that matter, Nashville, would be gathered again to the homeland, as King Cyrus of Persia had repatriated the Jews in Babylonian exile to Jerusalem. Still other Christians have concluded that all Jews today need to relocate to Israel in order for Jesus to return to the earth. Personally, I am not planning on leaving the United States.

Many of Jesus's early followers regarded themselves also as dispersed, but not from an earthly homeland. Rather, they saw themselves as pilgrims in the Diaspora now, but journeying to their heavenly homeland. In what is likely the New Testament's earliest document, 1 Thessalonians, Paul assures his audience about Jesus's return, *Then we, the ones living, the ones who are remaining, at the same time with them [the now-raised dead] will be snatched away in the clouds to meet the Lord [kyrios] in the air* (1 Thessalonians 4:17). James (1:1) is addressed *to the twelve tribes in the Diaspora*. The First Epistle of Peter (1:1) is written *to the refugees of the Diaspora in Pontus, Galatia, Cappadocia, Asia, and Bithynia*.

The idea of this gathering of the elect provides us another prompt, this one in relation to where we feel at home. Do we imagine life on this earth as an extended hotel stay before we finally get home? Are we pilgrims, or have we already arrived at the end of the journey? The verse also makes me think of houses of worship where people, holding a common belief or celebrating a common identity, find themselves both gathered and at home.

> **The best one can do is "watch" and remain faithful and trust in divine mercy. The verdict of salvation is not up to us; it is up to God.**

The elect will be gathered. The verse is assuring. And yet, Mark, and I think Jesus as well, doesn't want us to be too comfortable. The parable of the sower reminds us that not all seeds have deep roots. Mark has already shown us that the disciples frequently misunderstand Jesus. As we move into the Passion Narrative in Mark 14–15, we encounter Judas who betrays him, Peter who denies him three times, and the other disciples who flee from the cross. The Gospel unsettles the question of insiders vs. outsiders. The best one can do is "watch" and remain faithful and trust in divine mercy. The verdict of salvation is not up to us; it is up to God.

CHAPTER 6

Judas Iscariot and the Naked Young Man

Mark 14–15

Mark's Gospel has been driving toward the Passion Narrative since chapter 8 when Jesus, speaking plainly, announces his rejection, suffering, death, and resurrection. To this point, his disciples have not acknowledged these predictions. Many years ago in a New Testament introduction course, I assigned Mark 1–8 as the reading for the first class and Mark 9–16 for the second. Midweek, an undergraduate called me on the office phone (you can tell how long ago this was; today, students text). "He died," she cried over the phone; "he died." The call not only demonstrates the lack of religious literacy among students today; it also shows what happens when readers identify with the disciples. Jesus's disciples did not believe he would die; neither did my student.

I think Mark would like us to accompany the disciples but then take the next steps: where they fail, Mark's audience—who from the beginning of the Gospel has known more than the characters in the Gospel—can continue.

I assured the student that although Mark's Gospel lacks resurrection appearances, she need not worry. When Jesus states in Mark 14:28, *after I am raised, I will go before you to the Galilee,* she can trust him. She was, she told me the next class, much relieved.

In this chapter we look at two figures to see what questions their portrayals prompt, and how answering those questions can help us better understand Mark's Gospel in its own time and in ours. We start with the insider, Judas Iscariot, who to this point has been a faithful disciple, or more accurately, has been as faithful, and as confused, as the other eleven. We then meet Mark's most enigmatic figure, an unidentified man who is with Jesus in Gethsemane, and who flees from the arrest, leaving his garment behind. He starts apparently as an insider, becomes an outsider, and then? We may, or may not, meet him again in Mark 16 and so the conclusion to this volume.

Judas Iscariot

Mark 14 begins with the notice of the plot by the chief priest and scribes to kill Jesus and then describes a woman who anoints Jesus's head with expensive oil, an anointing Jesus explains as being for his burial. Mark thereby sets up three parties: people who want to kill Jesus (chief priests and scribes), people who honor him (the woman who anoints him), and people who do not understand him (the others at table who question the use of expensive ointment rather than giving the money to the poor, the disciples). Mark thus asks the audience: To which party do you belong? Mark then asks again, are you sure? Thanks, Mark.

Immediately following this dinner, Mark introduces the betrayal. Mark 14:10-11 recounts:

> *And Judas Iscariot, one of the Twelve, went out to the chief priests so that him [Jesus] he might hand over to them. And when they heard, they rejoiced, and they promised to him silver to give, and he was seeking when him, at an good opportune time [Greek: eu-kairos], he might hand over.*

The placement of this notice, immediately after the anointing, sets up a contrast: the woman spends her money on Jesus; Judas will receive money from the priests. The placement also creates another intercalation, a sandwiched story. Mark 14 begins with the chief priests and scribes plotting Jesus's death; then the anointing in the middle; finally, a return of the chief priests, now connected to Judas and so to the fulfillment of their plans. The frame explains why Jesus needs to be anointed; it also confirms his earlier Passion predictions.

In presenting the second part of the narrative frame, Mark did not need to state that Judas was *one of the Twelve.* Mark 3:19 ends the list of the disciples with *and Judas Iscariot, who handed him over.* The Greek *paradidōmi* literally means "hand over" as in Romans 8:32, where Paul praises God for having *handed over* the Son and in 1 Corinthians 15:3, where Paul speaks of *handing over* to the Corinthians the teachings he had received. The term can also mean "betray," and that is how Mark uses it here. When we pass something along—teaching, news, gossip—we might question whether we are being faithful transmitters, or whether we are betraying the source.

Despite the notice of Judas's betrayal in Mark 3:19, from then until chapter 15, Judas does not stand out, either for his missionary success or his failure to understand Jesus. He's been with us all along, but with Mark's greater attention to Peter, James, and John, he's easy to forget.

Mark does not tell us whether Judas always intended to betray Jesus, or whether the anointing, with that apparent waste of perfume, caused him to reject Jesus's mission and message. That Judas was evil from the start is the view John's Gospel follows. John 12:4-6 indicates both that Judas was the one who asked at a dinner about giving the money to the poor and that Judas really wanted to steal the money for himself.

Nor does Mark tell us that when Jesus appointed Judas to be among the Twelve, he knew about the betrayal. At times Jesus appears omniscient, as in Mark 13 where he predicts the "what" if not the "when" of the Second Coming, or when he reads the minds of his opponents (e.g., Mark 2:8, where Jesus was *knowing in his spirit* that the scribes were questioning his claims to forgive sin).

How we understand Judas thus impacts how we understand Jesus: did Jesus appoint Judas to facilitate the betrayal? If he did, is Jesus partially responsible for Judas's actions?

Alternatively, is Judas himself possessed by Satan, which is what both Luke 22:3 and John 13:2 propose, such that his actions are not his own?

Another explanation for the handing over is to see Judas as attempting to motivate Jesus to act. Jesus has already momentarily stopped business in the Temple, so he's capable of public action. He's already taught in the Temple, so he's capable of public debate. Is Judas trying to get him to state publicly that he is the son of David, the king of Israel? An ancient text, perhaps as early as the late second century, known as the Gospel of Judas, suggests that Jesus asked Judas to hand him over. Thus, Judas is not a betrayer but a colluder.

Some readers cast Judas as a Zealot, a revolutionary seeking to promote violence against Rome. There is no hint of this view in the Gospels, although it does work nicely in screenplays.

Nor can we be certain what exactly Judas betrayed. Mark's plot suggests that he betrayed where Jesus could be found, apart from the crowd. Could there be more? When Peter finally recognizes Jesus's identity and proclaims him to the be Christ (the Messiah), Jesus *strongly rebuked them not anyone to speak about him* (Mark 8:29-30). Thus, for some commentators, what Judas betrays is not only Jesus's location but also that Jesus has messianic pretentions or, by extension, wants to be the Davidic king.

Mark, by leaving Judas's motive and Jesus's knowledge unstated, demands more from us readers.

Given that Mark is writing in the first century, when the followers of Jesus were a minority whose views are rejected by majority Jewish as well as Gentile communities, perhaps Mark is warning readers: there may be a Judas among you. In the previous chapter (13:12), Jesus warned his followers about betrayal (using *paradidōmi* language) within the family: siblings will turn on siblings, parents on children and children on parents. Now Mark tells us that Jesus himself understands this rejection. Not only does Judas reject him, Judas also betrays him.

Popular culture focuses upon Judas's payment of thirty pieces of silver. That's Matthew 26:15, where Judas asks the chief priests what they will give him for handing Jesus over. Mark mentions neither greed as a motive nor, in the initial conversation, the amount. I would feel better if I knew the motive. Without motive, Judas seems to me more dangerous. Is he a political agitator, a greedy schemer, or a sociopath? Does the motive matter? Does the motive change our understanding of him, or is he beyond understanding, or redemption?

We next meet Judas at the Last Supper. Here is Mark 14:17-21:

> *And evening having occurred, he [Jesus] came with the Twelve. And when they are reclining at table, and they are eating, Jesus said, "Amen, I say to you, that one of you will betray me, the one eating with me." And they began to be grieved/in pain and to say to him one and then one [one after another], "No way I." And he said to them, "One of the Twelve, the one dipping with me into the bowl. Because on the one hand, the Son of Humanity goes away just as it is written about him, but woe to that person through whom the Son of Humanity is betrayed/handed over; better to him if not had been born that one."*

Jesus has arranged to celebrate the Passover. *And evening having occurred, he came with the Twelve.* Judas's meeting with the chief priests and scribes has gone undetected by the other disciples. Then Jesus betrays Judas's secret, *And when they are reclining at table, and they are eating, Jesus said, "Amen, I say to you, that one of you will hand me over, the one eating with me"* (Mark 14:17). Mid-meal, he makes a formal pronouncement.

Sympathetic commentators suggest that Jesus was being vague to prompt Judas to confess. It's a nice idea, but I doubt this is what

Mark, or Jesus, had in mind. Mark has already told us that Judas would betray Jesus. Moreover, were the issue to prompt a confession, the better move would have been to take Judas aside and speak to him privately.

Other commentators suggest that Jesus is asking all Twelve to consider their commitment to him: will they stay faithful, or not? This alternative strikes me as a better reading. We are all capable of loyalty and betrayal, supreme good and supreme evil. Jesus is about to institute the memorial meal in his name, what has come to be called Communion or the Eucharist. One might want to examine one's motives before coming to what has become known as the Lord's Table.

Jesus knew that he would be betrayed, and he knew who would betray him. We do not know when he realized, but he knew. He does nothing to stop Judas. Nor does he tell his other disciples what Judas plans to do. I've had chats with Mark about this situation. According to Leviticus 19, the same chapter in which we are commanded to love our neighbors as ourselves (19:18) and to love the strangers who dwell among us (19:34), we are also commanded to reprove our sinful neighbors openly so that we do not find ourselves guilty of sin as well (19:17). To be aware of a crime and to do nothing to stop it brings guilt. Jesus knew that Judas was about to betray him: he should have said something; he should have done something. I am sympathetic to Judas. Should I be?

Jesus's comment about the one dining with him also alludes to earlier Scripture. Psalm 41, a psalm of the lament of an individual and ascribed to King David (like Psalm 22 which begins, *My God, my God, why have you forsaken me?*) describes the betrayal of a close friend, *whom I trusted, who ate my bread.*

The disciples react: *And they began to be grieved/in pain and to say to him one and then one (one after another), "No way I."* Mark does not tell us whether Judas, too, was grieved. Perhaps he was. Perhaps he felt compelled to do what he had planned to do. Was he following a divine plan, and if so, then I've got complaints against God. Was he committed to the action and did not think he could back out? If so, I've got complaints against Judas just as I have complaints about Herod Antipas, who has John the Baptizer killed in the context of a meal. Both Judas and Antipas could have refused to go through with the plan. Before the deed is done, no matter how meticulous the planning, there is time to stop.

Finally, Jesus says to his disciples that the betrayer is *the one dipping with me into the bowl.* Did the other eleven now know that the one to hand him over was Judas? Was Jesus asking for help, or stating what must happen? Should they have acted, or were they recalling Jesus's rebuke of Peter back in Caesarea Philippi? Mark tells us nothing. Nothing. Mark leaves us at the table, looking at each other. Do we trust? Do we damn? What do we do, or say?

This scene ends with Jesus pronouncing the inevitability of what will occur: *the Son of Humanity goes away just as it is written about him* (14:21). There is no Scripture that explicitly states that the Son of Humanity or the Messiah would be handed over. The verse may be Mark's way of signaling that whatever happened was determined. Paul records in 1 Corinthians 15:3-4 the teachings that had been handed over to him: *that Christ died for our sins according to the Scriptures.*

Then Jesus states, *But woe to the perspn through whom the Son of Humanity is betrayed/handed over; better to him if not had been born that one* (14:21). I have problems with this verse. When I mention my problems with this verse to my friends (I have very patient friends), they assure me that what happened was meant to be. One suggests that Judas is to be compared to Satan in Eden: had Satan not tempted Adam and Eve, they would never have eaten the forbidden fruit, and therefore Jesus never would have come to earth. I find this argument unconvincing. Another posits that Judas was like Joseph's brother Judah (this is the same name: Judas is Greek, and Judah is Hebrew), who sold Joseph to the Egyptians. An initial act of betrayal set up the circumstances by which Egypt and surrounding areas would be saved from famine. This seems a convoluted way of providing rescue; worse, it justifies bad behavior. A third, less theologically inclined, speaks of the human need for scapegoats, for someone to blame for our own shortcomings. A fourth even wonders if Judas existed, since according to Paul it was God who handed Jesus over.

I wrestle with the idea that anyone is predestined to do evil. If we are programmed, I want Judas to pray, as Jesus does, *take this cup away from me* (Mark 14:36). Or if Judas has no motive but is a sociopath, then we still need to see him in the divine image and likeness. And if he is, as Luke and John propose, possessed by Satan, like that fellow from Gerasa, he needs our pity and our compassion, not our scorn.

Mark does not tell us when Judas departs to tell the chief priests where they can find Jesus. The scene turns to the Eucharist, in which, apparently, Judas participates. In instituting this meal, Jesus tells the disciples that the wine is the *blood of the covenant, which is poured out for many* (Mark 14:24). He does not say, as he does in Matthew 26:28, that the blood is for "the forgiveness of sins." I wonder if this addition would have made a difference to Judas.

The group then departs for the Mount of Olives, where Jesus tells them that they *will all stumble* (from the Greek *skandalidzō*, where we get the word "scandalized"), *for it is written, 'I will strike the shepherd, and the sheep will be scattered'* (Mark 14:27). Peter insists not only that he will remain faithful, but even if he has to die with Jesus, he will never deny him. Mark 14:31 adds that the other disciples said the same thing. Judas, if he has not left yet, would be among the group. Despite promises, we all fail at some point. The question is how we fail: like Judas, without a look back, or like Peter, with regret and repentance? The next question is how those whom we fail look at us. Could we, like Jesus (I am imagining here) look at Peter with love? Could we, or he, do the same for Judas, as he did for that rich young man (here we may recall Mark 10:21)?

In Gethsemane, Jesus prays in the agony of knowing that he will be crucified. Three times he asks his inner circle of Peter, James, and John to keep watch with him; three times they fall asleep. Finally, he rouses them. Here is Judas's last appearance in the Gospel, Mark 14:42-46:

Rise up, let us go. Look, the one handing me over is near.

And immediately, yet while he was speaking, appeared Judas, one of the Twelve, and with him a crowd with swords and clubs, from the high priests and the scribes and the elders.

And had given, the one handing him over, a sign to them, saying, "Whomever I might kiss, he is, seize him, and lead him away, safely."

And as he was coming, immediately he was coming toward him, he says, "Rabbi," and he kissed him.

And they cast their hands on him and seized him.

By describing Judas both as *one of the Twelve,* and as being together with *a crowd with swords and clubs, from the high priests and the scribes and the elders* (14:43), Mark places him in what appear to be distinct groups. Mark again complicates the question of who is in and who is out.

The most perfidious of Judas's actions is the sign by which he hands Jesus over to the mob: *Whomever I might kiss, he is, seize him* (14:44). The kiss is an intimate act that marks relationships between parents and children (e.g., Genesis 31:28; 1 Kings 19:20) as well as between lovers (Song of Songs 1:2 and elsewhere). It is also the way the followers of Jesus, his new mother and brothers and sisters, greeted each other, as attested in Romans 16:16; 1 Corinthians 16:20; 2 Corinthians 13:12; 1 Thessalonians 5:26, and 1 Peter 5:14. I list all these examples to show how prominent the motif of greeting by what Paul calls a "holy kiss" and what 1 Peter calls a "kiss of love" is. Signs of discipleship can be false, and signs of love can hide acts of betrayal.

Judas then exacerbates the betrayal by addressing Jesus as *Rabbi,* as "my teacher." The only other person in the Gospel to use this address is Peter, once in 9:5, at the Metamorphosis, where he suggests making tents for Jesus, Elijah, and Moses, and again in 11:21 when he remarks at the withering of the fig tree. In the first instance, he does not understand what he is saying; in the second, he does not understand what he is seeing. What kind of rabbi, what kind of teacher, does he suppose Jesus to be? What kind of teacher should he think Jesus to be?

While the disciples, other than Judas, are not among those who arrest Jesus, it is possible some are armed. Mark 14:47 notes that someone at the arrest drew a sword and sliced off the ear of an enslaved man owned by the high priest (Luke 22:51 tells us that Jesus repaired the damaged ear). Today we call this collateral damage.

I am more worried about the person with the sword, since I do not know who he is. I suspect he may be one of the Twelve, or a sympathizer; on the other hand, he could have been a member of the party sent to arrest Jesus who got caught up in the moment. Was the violence random, or planned? The problems with insider-versus-outsider status thus continue: Can we tell the difference between defense and offense? More, what should the disciples have done? Should they go after Judas, and, if they catch him, what then? Berate him? Rough him up? Ask him to explain? Ask him to repent?

Judas betrays Jesus with a kiss and then departs from the story. We never see him collect the money; Mark makes no mention of the thirty pieces of silver. According to Matthew 27:5, Judas threw the silver in the Temple and then hanged himself. Matthew is drawing on 2 Samuel 17:23, where Ahithophel, David's advisor who threw in his lot with Absalom, realizing his cause is lost, hanged himself. Luke has Judas explode (Acts 1:18). For Mark, Judas's fate remains open.

Judas provides a warning against judging others, especially when we do not know their motives. Judas provides an opportunity to discuss the extent and the limits of forgiveness and reconciliation.

He opens the conversation about fate and freewill, predestination and control of our futures. Judas raises questions about Jesus's own complicity in allowing the betrayal to go forward, which is part of the larger conversation about why a good and gracious God allows evil in the world.

> **Judas raises questions about Jesus's own complicity in allowing the betrayal to go forward, which is part of the larger conversation about why a good and gracious God allows evil in the world.**

The Naked Young Man

According to Mark 14, after Judas betrays Jesus with a kiss and someone lops off an ear in the melee of the arrest, the following occurs. This is Mark 14:50-52, speaking initially of the disciples:

And leaving him, they all were fleeing.

And some young man was accompanying him, wearing upon nakedness a linen cloth/shroud, and they seized him. And leaving the linen cloth/shroud, naked he fled.

This scene should not, as far as my literary taste goes, be here. I want to know what happens to Judas, I want to know what happens to Peter whose three-time denial has yet to be documented, and I want attention to be focused on Jesus who has just been arrested. The final scene in Mark 14 seems to me out of place. Yet given Mark's tendency of keeping readers off balance, these reactions of "Who?" and "What?" and "Huh?" are on the mark. The Gospel leaves this young man as a mystery, an invitation to readers to do something with him or learn something from him. I'll follow the various clues with you and give you some suggestions. But, as the end of the

Gospel requires the readers to fill in the next scenes, so with this young man, we readers must determine for ourselves how his story ends and what it means.

My first inclination is to see the young man as among the disciples, since just as Jesus had predicted his death, he predicted the disciples' desertion. Their flight is the culmination of their failures. Consistently they have misunderstood him. Peter, James, and John fall asleep three times rather than remain awake and so comfort Jesus as he prays (Mark 14:37, 40, 41). Except for Peter, this is the last appearance of the once Twelve, now minus Judas, the Eleven. But maybe the category of "disciple" is broader than just Twelve. Maybe we can include Levi the tax collector or the women who followed Jesus from Galilee.

Mark states that not only did they flee the arrest, but also the disciples were *leaving him*. The verb I translate "leaving," *aphiēmi*, can also mean "to desert," "to abandon," and "to forsake." The verb is common, but how Mark uses it elsewhere can impact how we read chapter 14. In certain cases it can also mean "to forgive" in the sense of "to let go." In Mark 1:18 *aphiēmi* describes how Peter and Andrew "left" their nets to follow Jesus. Abandoning a job is already a huge step in discipleship. Next, Jesus calls James and John, and *immediately they left [aphiēmi] their father Zebedee in the boat* (Mark 1:20). The disciples abandoned Jesus, just as they abandoned their father. We can imagine how Zebedee felt and now we realize Jesus understands that same feeling. *Aphiēmi* is not, however, the term Jesus uses in his cry from the cross, *My God, my God, why have you forsaken me* (Mark 15:34).

The disciples, except for Judas, at some point regrouped. According to Matthew 28:16-20, the Eleven reunited with Jesus in Galilee, where he had promised to meet them (Mark 14:28; Matthew 26:32; Matthew also has an angel at the tomb, and then Jesus himself, tell the women that he will meet the disciples in Galilee; see Matthew 28:7-10). At the end of the Gospel Matthew 28:16-20 takes the prediction and provides it a fulfillment. John and Luke set the reunion scenes initially in Jerusalem. Mark, without a reconstitution of the disciples and without a Resurrection appearance, requires us to move beyond the Gospel's end and to finish the story ourselves. The fidelity of the reader fills the gap left by the disciples' flight. We feel their fear, and their despair, and yet we persevere.

> **Mark, without a reconstitution of the disciples and without a Resurrection appearance, requires us to move beyond the Gospel's end and to finish the story ourselves.**

Now our mysterious figure: *And some young man was accompanying him* (14:51). Unnamed, this young man (*neaniskos*) takes his place alongside the numerous other unnamed characters in Mark's Gospel: Peter's mother-in-law, the fellow healed of paralysis, the hemorrhaging and now dried-up woman, Jairus's daughter, the anointing woman, the centurion at the cross, and many others.

It is possible our young man represents all those other unnamed disciples who supported the mission. He stayed, apparently longer than did the named disciples, but in the end, he, too, flees. He could symbolize the disciples, in that he is left with nothing: not even a piece of clothing. Like the Twelve, he too fails, but he, too, may get a second chance following the Resurrection.

Occasionally, biblical scholars suggest that this young man is the writer Mark himself, and that he has put in a personal appearance, just as Alfred Hitchcock has cameos in his movies. While this view can explain how the author came to learn what happened in Gethsemane, I'm unconvinced.

It would be grand were Mark to have used the term for "young man," *neaniskos*, in describing the potential disciple whom Jesus loved and to whom he advised selling all and giving the proceeds to the poor (Mark 10:21-22). Matthew 19:20 uses the term *neaniskos* for the rich fellow, but not Mark. I like the idea of this naked fellow as the one with whom Jesus earlier spoke: then we would have had a story in which discipleship comes after some thought, and in which technically he gives up "all he had."

Luke 7:14 uses the term *neaniskos* for the son of the widow of Nain, whom Jesus raises from the dead. Mark does not contain this story. The term identifies Paul's nephew in Acts 23, but a connection of Paul's nephew to Mark's young man would be unlikely.

However, Mark does use this identification of *neaniskos* one more time. In Mark 16:5, we, along with Mary Magdalene, Mary the mother of Joses, and Salome, meet a *neaniskos* at Jesus's empty tomb. The same young man as the one who fled naked from the arrest? We'll return to this figure in the conclusion. For now, more on his appearance in Mark 14.

Our young man was *wearing upon nakedness a linen cloth/ shroud* (14:51). Most people at the time had two garments, an inner and an outer. An outer garment, such as a cloak, could indicate a comparably higher status. In his commissioning of the Twelve, Jesus commands them *not to put on two tunics* (Mark 6:9). That this fellow had only one garment and otherwise was naked could indicate that he was poor, that he was a high-status individual who divested, or that perhaps he had come to Jesus in the hopes of being baptized, or again that he heard the commotion and ran out of his house without taking time to dress. But I think we are more likely with this fellow to find meaning if we look at his garment, and his nakedness, as having symbolic value.

The reference to his nakedness (*gymnos*, whence "gymnasium") conveys several mutually exclusive impressions. It can indicate poverty, as in the famous parable of the sheep and the goats, where Jesus says, *I was naked, and you clothed me* (Matthew 25:36). Or, it can indicate the innocence associated with the garden of Eden, where the man and the woman were naked, and they were not ashamed

(Genesis 2:25; I heard an alternative translation, that Adam and Eve were naked, and were not disappointed; I like that option, although I doubt it's what the author of Genesis intended). It's too bad Mark does not describe Gethsemane as a garden; that description is from John 18:1, 26. Perhaps we should see him as a newborn, having to start a new life without the physical presence of Jesus. Or, to extend the reference, nakedness can indicate both birth and death. In Job 1:21, the eponymous narrator famously states, *Naked I went out from the womb of my mother, and naked I shall return there. The Lord* [YHWH] *gave, and the Lord* [YHWH] *took; let be the name of the Lord* [YHWH] *blessed.* Or again, when one entered the miqveh (ritual bath) to restore purity, one was nude, and this was probably the case for those who presented themselves to John for baptism in the Jordan. The youth's nakedness is an open symbol, and you may have your own takeaway (as it were) for what it signifies.

The reference to his nudity remains open; so does the reference to the garment. The fellow is wearing a *sindon*, a linen cloth. This is not local homespun but linen, which was often imported, whether from India or Egypt. The young man is a walking contradiction: the poverty of nakedness coupled with the wealth of linen.

Making matters more complicated, *sindon* also means a shroud. According to Mark 15:46, Joseph of Arimathea purchases a *sindon* for the body of Jesus. The connection of the youth's nakedness to birth and death becomes stronger with this connotation of his garment.

We next learn that the arresting party perceived the young man to be with Jesus, *and they seized him.* Why not seize any of the eleven named disciples? Judas was there; he could have said, "Over there, those are James and John; get them."

The officers do to the youth exactly what they do to Jesus, they *seized* him. If the young man can escape, does that mean that Jesus himself will escape? That he could have escaped?

Mark ends the young man's story: *And leaving the linen cloth/ shroud, naked he fled.* In Mark 10:28, Peter said to Jesus, "Look, we have left everything and followed you." Here in Mark 14, we find someone who followed Jesus and then left everything, or at least everything he had with him. But he fled rather than followed. Had he remained with Jesus, also in custody, I would have more sympathy for him. And yet, perhaps like the Eleven, he represents the future faithful.

Biblical scholars, as we've noted, look to the earlier Scriptures for help in interpretation. For example, Amos 2:16 describes what happens when the people reject the prophets, "those who are stout of heart among the mighty / shall flee away naked on that day." I see the connection with nakedness and flight, but it does not much help me with what Mark is trying to convey. "On that day" for Amos is the judgment day; do we see Gethsemane as a type of judgment, and yet one in which failed and fleeing disciples get a do-over? Are we to have sympathy for our young man, since the arrest is a dangerous situation when even the mighty cannot withstand the pressure?

I do wish I had secure answers, but Mark prompts me to ask more and more questions, and with each question and answer, my assessment of this young man, and his garment, and his nakedness, changes.

To understand our mysterious figure, two more facts need to be entered into evidence. First, there is a literary motif of people leaving their garments behind. The most famous biblical example is Joseph. In Genesis 39, Jacob's son Joseph is purchased by Potiphar, an Egyptian officer (the term describing him in Hebrew is *saris*; the LXX reads *eunouchos*, "eunuch"). Potiphar's wife, finding Joseph exceedingly attractive, attempts, repeatedly, to seduce him. On one occasion, when the two are alone in the house, *She seized him, his garment, saying, 'Lie with me!' But he left his garment in her hand and fled* (Genesis 39:12). Mrs. Potiphar will use this garment as evidence that Joseph had attempted to seduce her. A fleeing naked young man: Is our fellow in Gethsemane like Joseph, innocent, but one to be humiliated (as Joseph is cast into prison) before he can be redeemed? Making the connection of Joseph to the young man at the arrest even more intriguing, two chapters earlier, in Genesis 37, Jacob's other sons dip Joseph's "coat of many colors" (or, less colorfully but more accurately, "long sleeved tunic") into the blood of a goat and present it to their father; Jacob concludes that Joseph had been devoured by wild animals. Joseph's brothers later see him wearing Egyptian clothing and fail to recognize him. A garment suggests death when the owner is alive. New clothing suggests new identity. Humiliation leading to exaltation, a happy ending. How much does Mark want us to recall about Joseph when we think about this young man in Gethsemane, and about the fate of Jesus?

The garment left in the hands of the arresting officer, given these earlier biblical motifs, cries out for interpretation. Is it a sign of divesting of goods, or divesting of life? Does it indicate awareness of having done the wrong thing, as Adam and Eve flee naked from God? Does the man represent anyone, faced with the choice of whether to accept or to deny Jesus, stripped of every conceit and deceit? In the presence of Jesus, are we fully exposed?

> **The garment left in the hands of the arresting officer, given these earlier biblical motifs, cries out for interpretation. Is it a sign of divesting of goods, or divesting of life?**

Second, and more controversial, is the relation of this scene to what has come to be called The Secret Gospel of Mark. You are welcome to look up details about this text on your own, but the short version is as follows. Morton Smith, a Columbia University professor, reported to have found at the Greek Orthodox Mar Saba monastery in Israel a text by Clement of Alexandria, a second-century Christian author, recording a version of Mark's Gospel. This text, which draws upon John 11, the raising of Lazarus, states that Jesus encountered a young man (*neaniskos*) whom Jesus raised from the dead, whom Jesus loved. The Secret Gospel then states, "in the evening, the youth comes to him, wearing a linen cloth (*sindon*) over this naked body," and that this youth "remained with him that night, for Jesus taught him the mystery of the Kingdom of God."

Biblical scholars and church historians continue to debate the Secret Gospel: Does it shed light on Mark's Gospel? Is it an ancient forgery? Is it a modern forgery? I mention it here not to resolve the numerous questions it raises (alas, I cannot), but to show how controversial biblical interpretation can be. But we cannot, at least in the academic community, discuss our naked young man without a reference to this controversial text.

> **Attempting to understand Jesus— the Son of Humanity who will come with the clouds of heaven, the tortured figure who cries from the cross, My God, my God, why have you forsaken me—we will never know all that we want to know.**

In the end, the naked young man eludes definitive interpretation. The young man who flees, naked, when Jesus is arrested, seems to me the perfect figure for the reader. Mark has stripped us of what we think we know, including what the later Gospels of Matthew, Luke, and John record. Attempting to understand Jesus—the Son of Humanity who will come with the clouds of heaven, the tortured figure who cries from the cross, *My God, my God, why have you forsaken me*—we will never know all that we want to know. At best we see, as Paul puts it, "through a glass, darkly" (KJV) or *through a mirror dimly* (1 Corinthians 13:12). Jesus remains mysterious but compelling; all powerful and tortured victim; fully God and fully human.

In Mark 14, we have the last appearance of Judas. Tradition insists on his degradation, although Mark leaves his future open. Can one repent from such a betrayal? Can we trust Judas again? Can we forgive him? In Mark 14, we have the naked young man fleeing from the arresting officers. Will he join the eleven disciples and continue in fidelity to Jesus, or will he flee also from the Gospel? Do we see ourselves in his role, stripped of anything that would prevent discipleship? As a naked newborn, does he get to start again? As a naked corpse, can he find himself reborn? Mark poses the challenge; it is our role to determine the response.

CONCLUSION

Most biblical scholars agree that the Gospel of Mark ends at 16:8, the flight of the women from the tomb. The text begins with reference to the women who witnessed the death of Jesus. Mark 15:40 reads, *and there were even women, from afar, watching, among whom even Mary the Magdalene/Mary the Tower, and Mary, she [the mother] of James the younger and Joses, and Salome.* I've left both names as "Mary": the Greek reads *Maria.*

The name "Magdalene" comes from the Hebrew word *migdal,* meaning "tower"; the name also refers to the city known from Talmudic sources as Magdala Nunayyaon, meaning "Tower of Fishes," which was located on the Sea of Galilee. Our Mary may well be named for this city, which was known for preserving fish by salting and then for exporting the product. If the geographical identification is correct, then Mary might have encountered Jesus through other people in the fishing industry, such as Peter and Andrew, James and John. We might also think of her name not only or even as indicating her hometown. Perhaps she was known as Mary the Tower, as Simon bar Jonah becomes known as Peter (from Greek *petros,* meaning "rock") or James and John are known as Boangerges, which Mark translates as "sons of thunder" (Mark 3:17).

The second Mary, here connected to James, could be the mother of Jesus, since Jesus had a brother named James. If so, however, this is an odd way of identifying her. Salome could be a sister of Jesus or the mother of the apostles James and John. Others suggest she is the "wife of Clopas" mentioned in John 19:25. Since "Mary" and "Salome" were the two most common names for Jewish women in late Second Temple Galilee and Judea, all we can do is speculate.

Conclusion

Mark 15:41 tells us that the women at the cross had been following Jesus since his days in Galilee and that they had come up with him to Jerusalem.

These women provide the continuity between the cross and the burial and so guarantee that the empty tomb is, in fact, the tomb in which Joseph of Arimathea placed Jesus's corpse. Thus, Mark 15:47 states, *And Mary the Magdalene/Mary the Tower, and Mary, she [the mother] of Joses were watching where he had been put.*

Mark 16 begins with the notice, *When had passed the Sabbath, Mary the Magdalene/Mary the Tower, and Mary, she [the mother] of James, and Salome brought aromatics, so that they might go and anoint him* (Mark 16:1). It is not the case, contrary to popular belief, that only women prepared corpses. However, the women here remind us of the unnamed woman who anointed Jesus's head the week before. When those at the table with him criticized her lavishing Jesus with expensive ointment rather than using the money to support the poor, Jesus responded that she had anointed his body for his burial (Mark 14:8). Thus, the women who go to the tomb are redundant; his body had already been prepared for its burial.

Again, Mark dislodges complacency based on insider status. The unnamed woman anointed Jesus's body, and he explains that she did so anticipating his death; these three named women, who had been following him from the Galilee and had heard his Passion predictions, did not believe he would be raised. They come to anoint a corpse. The three named women may be compared to the three named disciples—Peter, James, and John—at the Metamorphosis and at Gethsemane, who misunderstand Jesus and then fail him and then flee. Their counterpart, the unexpected outsider who understands the necessity for Jesus to suffer and die, is the unnamed centurion at the cross, who in Mark 15:39, at Jesus's death, proclaims, *Truly this man was a son of God.*

The three women in Mark 16 are not only redundant, they are also poor planners. Mark 16:2-3 states, *And exceedingly (early) in the morning, on the first (day) of the Sabbath, they came upon the tomb, having risen the sun. And they were saying to each other, "Who will roll away for us the stone from the door of the tomb?"* They realize moving the stone will be beyond their capacity, but why not go get someone stronger? I get the impression that they did not contact the male disciples, who perhaps had started to make their way back to the Galilee. Did the men return to meet Jesus? Did they return to their homes and families and jobs?

And looking up, they saw that had been rolled away the stone, for it was very large (16:4). Mark does not tell us what they would have thought at that sight. I suspect, were they not shocked into an inability to think, they would have been worried about graverobbers. Nails used to affix victims to crosses were considered to have magical properties. But the women, showing courage, persevere. *And entering into the tomb, they saw a young man (neaniskos), sitting on the right side, dressed in a white robe, and they were alarmed* (16:5). I would be too.

I am struck with how difficult this scene is to comprehend. Is this young man the same young man who ran naked from Gethsemane? Could our fleeing young man have been an angel in disguise, and now, wearing white garments as Jesus wore at the Metamorphosis (Mark 9:3) in his original state? When we see him, are we to think that this is what the risen Jesus looks like?

And he says to them, "Do not be alarmed. Jesus, you are seeking, the Nazarene, the one having been crucified, is risen. Not is he here. See the site where they put him" (16:6). The young man makes explicit three key points. First, the women are in fact at the correct tomb. Thus, Mark assures us that the women did not go to the wrong tomb. Second, Jesus was crucified and thus he in fact died. Third, he has risen not as a disembodied spirit, but is, in fact, in his own, now transformed body. Without these three points, the tomb is only empty space: alone, it proves nothing.

Conclusion

The young man then commands the women, *But go, say to his disciples and to Peter that, 'He goes before you into the Galilee; there you will see him, just as he said to you'"* (16:7). Numerous commentators then suggest, incorrectly, that Jewish law forbids women from serving as witnesses, so that the commission to the women to testify breaks tradition. The women are not testifying in a court of law. Moreover, they are to report what they have seen and heard to their associates, not to the public. The young man's command rather alludes to Mark 14:28, Jesus's comment to his disciples as they move from the Last Supper to the Mount of Olives and then to Gethsemane, *After I am raised, I will go ahead of you to the Galilee.* Were the women with him when he made this comment? If so, they were likely with him at the Last Supper and at Gethsemane as well.

The good news of Jesus's resurrection is ready to be proclaimed.

But not in Mark's Gospel. Mark leaves that task to readers, then and now. The last line of the original text is, *And going out, they fled from the tomb, for they were trembling and outside themselves* [Greek: *ek-stasis*], *and to no one nothing did they say, for they were afraid* (16:8). The double negative in Greek, "to no one nothing" is an intensification: they said nothing, not anything, to anyone. The Gospel ends with frightened, silent women fleeing from the empty tomb. We seem to be back at Gethsemane... the fear, the flight, left with nothing.

Mark gives us no Resurrection appearance, but Mark assures readers that Jesus will meet his followers in Galilee. Jesus correctly predicted his death, and Mark's readers, after 70, know that he also correctly predicted the destruction of the Jerusalem Temple. The disciples in Mark fail, but we know from other New Testament sources and indeed from the history of the church, that they returned, regrouped, and repented. Jesus cried from the cross, *My God, my God, why have you forsaken me?* We know that this is the first verse of Psalm 22, a psalm that ends with the universal acclamation of divine glory. We readers must fill in the rest of the story.

The last verses of the Torah's fifth book, Deuteronomy, record the death of Moses (Deuteronomy 34:5-12). When we Jews read the Torah and reach the end, on the holiday called Simchat Torah, "Rejoicing in/with Torah," we rewind the scroll and begin again with Genesis 1:1, *When, in the beginning, God created the heavens and the earth.* We start again, knowing the end of the story and knowing what we have done in the past year, and we learn anew. Each year we return to the beginning, and each time we see new things.

> **We start again, knowing the end of the story and knowing what we have done in the past year, and we learn anew. Each year we return to the beginning, and each time we see new things.**

The young man sends the women and the disciples back to the Galilee, where we can follow them, not in the text, but in our imagination. We are back to where we saw John immersing people in the Jordan and preparing them for the Messiah's arrival. Again, we hear the parable of the sower, and so we check for the depth of our roots and for thorns in our way. We are back in a place of miracles and exorcisms, and of the death of the Baptizer. We travel again with Jesus to Caesarea Philippi and to the Mount of the Metamorphosis, where we first hear the prediction of the cross and only now, ever briefly, see Jesus in full messianic glory. We reread Mark 13, the Little Apocalypse, and locate ourselves in this in-between time, between the Resurrection and the end of the world, which is surely coming, although we cannot ever know when. We watch Judas do what he must do and consider again our own potential for both fidelity and failure. We watch the youth flee from Gethsemane, and then, maybe, see him again at the tomb. We listen for the women's voices, and when they do not speak, we fill in the story, Jesus's story, and our story, again. Each time we pass through the Gospel it is not the same, for we are not the same. Each time we are confronted with new mysteries and challenges; each time we find partial answers and temporary comfort.

> **Each time we pass through the Gospel it is not the same, for we are not the same.**

Mark makes us work harder than Matthew, Luke, and John, but in making us do the work, Mark also makes us better readers and better disciples. Mark introduces us to the mysterious Son of Humanity, fully human and fully divine; just when we think we completely understand him, we are back at the beginning to try again.

The fear and the silence of the women is never the last word. Mark leaves us the time, and the space, to make our own proclamations.

**Watch videos based
on *The Gospel of Mark:
A Beginner's Guide to
the Good News*
with Amy-Jill Levine
through Amplify Media.**

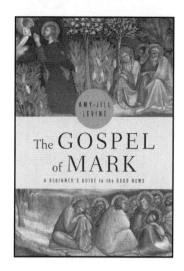

Amplify Media is a multimedia platform that delivers high quality, searchable content with an emphasis on Wesleyan perspectives for churchwide, group, or individual use on any device at any time. In a world of sometimes overwhelming choices, Amplify gives church leaders and congregants media capabilities that are contemporary, relevant, effective and, most importantly, affordable and sustainable.

With *Amplify Media* church leaders can:

- Provide a reliable source of Christian content through a Wesleyan lens for teaching, training, and inspiration in a customizable library
- Deliver their own preaching and worship content in a way the congregation knows and appreciates
- Build the church's capacity to innovate with engaging content and accessible technology
- Equip the congregation to better understand the Bible and its application
- Deepen discipleship beyond the church walls

**Ask your group leader or pastor about Amplify Media
and sign up today at www.AmplifyMedia.com.**

Made in the USA
Columbia, SC
14 September 2023

22872838R00098